Are we there Yet?

How to keep going when Christian living gets real

Ruth Baker

Ark House Press
PO Box 1722, Port Orchard, WA 98366 USA
PO Box 1321, Mona Vale NSW 1660 Australia
PO Box 318 334, West Harbour, Auckland 0661 New Zealand
arkhousepress.com

© Ruth Baker 2020

Unless otherwise stated, all Scriptures are taken from the New Living Translation (Holy Bible. New Living Translation copyright© 1996, 2004, 2007, 2013 by Tyndale House Foundation. Used by permission of Tyndale House Publishers Inc., Carol Stream, Illinois 60188. All rights reserved.)

Some names and identifying details have been changed to protect the privacy of individuals.

Cataloguing in Publication Data:
Title: Are We There Yet?
ISBN: 978-0-6488259-9-9 (pbk)
Subjects: Christian Living;

Design by initiateagency.com

For Kathryn, Nissa, Sharon and Julie who keep me sane and grounded. And for William and Henry who are the best travelling companions of all.

Chapter 1
The beginning of our journey

I didn't become a Christian until I was in my thirties, and when I met Jesus, it was like someone had switched a light on and I didn't realise until that moment that I'd been stumbling about in the dark. For me, it was a two-stage conversion. I became a Christian in my head first and about a year later, in my heart as well.

I became a believer because the more I learned, the more I realised it was more probably true than not. When I learned the evidence around the resurrection of Jesus Christ, I became a Christian. The evidence was too compelling for it to not be true. And if that was true, well... the only thing you can do is give your life to Jesus.

About a year later, I was at a large conference and with hundreds of women's voices raised in song, I suddenly got it. What had happened in my head the year before, suddenly happened in my heart too. I got it. I suddenly understood the very depth of my sin and therefore the extent of gratitude I owed to God.

Both stages were life changing and in both stages I felt like I had an enormous spiritual growth spurt. The first stage, while intellectual, was like being a "Christian toddler". My understanding was small, but I was learning and growing. I felt like I had so much to learn, and my main concern was, if I am a Christian, what am I supposed to *do*? The second stage brought me into what felt like my spiritual young adult years. My heart had been changed and I was asking more questions. Now, my pre-occupation was with what I was doing as a *response*. I had experienced the grace of God. Everything you do in obedience is in gratitude to that deep truth.

In these early years, I was running one hundred miles per hour. I wanted to learn and grow so that, come the day when I faced God, he would welcome me as his good and faithful servant. I wanted to know God. I wanted to purify my dark heart which, until then, had beaten so sinfully. So even though I was responding to God's grace, that still meant doing things. In fact, I knew I needed to *do* things so that my heart was moulded and shaped anew.

And do what? Most sermons give a good "what's next" application at the end. We should read our Bibles, pray, serve in ministry, give financially to the church and spread the gospel. We should do these things frequently and faithfully. How we do them and how we integrate them into real life is a matter of much mental and logistical wrestling.

I'd read more books and listen to talks and go to conferences to try and get that perfect balance – and always coming up short of what I thought I should be doing. I couldn't seem to get it right. Or, I could "get it right" (based on what I thought I should be doing) but then not be able to keep it up. The talks and conferences largely left me confused and disappointed in myself.

What we need, I thought, is a guide to help us do this Christian living thing. We need something to help us challenge our expectations of ourselves and get back to what is biblical. At the same time, we need help to keep going with our discipleship, because the Christian journey doesn't look like we think it should look like.

I want to live this life well and live it for Jesus, but I find that I am hampered by my expectations of what I should be doing, and what level of excellence it should display. On top of that, sometimes my energy doesn't keep up with even basic expectations. How am I supposed to do life then? Add to that filling my head with talks and books and conferences and suddenly I don't know what I'm supposed think or do next.

If you are anything like me, then this bothers you too. It may bother you that when we hear in a sermon that we should keep our eyes fixed on Jesus, we don't know what that looks like in practice. You might be the kind of person who looks at others in church and thinks they have it all together and your Christian journey is bumpy at best. You might wonder – How do I stay focused? How do I stay obedient?

We have a picture in our heads of what a Christian is supposed to look like – and it's rarely what our life looks like. The Christians who look like I think they're supposed to, well, they're just so perfect. Me? I'm horribly mediocre. I'm so ordinary. I don't know how I'm supposed to do this Christian journey thing.

Well, this book is where we get to come together to re-look at this. We are going to be challenging our assumptions and our actions and our thinking. But we're going to look at this together, so we all have a better handle on this. This is guide for all of us, together, as we face real life, under God.

Even Paul wasn't perfect

Even Paul in his letter to the Philippians pointed out that he was ordinary:

"Not that I have already obtained all this, or have already arrived at my goal, but I press on to take hold of that for which Christ Jesus took hold of me." (Philippians 3:12) He's been talking to the Philippians about faith and its expression in their day to day lives. And he tells them not even he is a perfect Christian. And yet this picture persists of all the things we should be doing and how we aren't doing them. This leaves me feeling that I'm a massive loser and now my brain hurts and I want to cry.

Let's all take a collective breath.

There is a great irony here. You see we *are* losers. Paul had also said *"I consider everything a loss because of the surpassing worth of knowing Christ Jesus my Lord."* (Philippians 3:8)

This alone should put our view of what it looks like to be a Christian in perspective. We know Christ Jesus our Lord. Everything else is loss. We are saved. Not because of some list of Christian do's and don'ts that we think we should be doing. We are saved through God's grace alone, through faith in Christ alone. That's it. That's all.

So why bother worrying about how we're living as Christians? And whether we're meeting expectations? Because we're still human. Being concerned about how we are living isn't about trying to earn salvation. It is an expression of our hearts as they change and are shaped into an increasing Christlikeness. The Spirit guides and enables us, but we still need to exercise our will and wisdom. We still need to make good choices on the basis of knowing God and our growing discipleship in Christ. And that's difficult.

We aren't alone in being concerned about how we live now that we're Christians. Most of Paul's letters deal with this very thing: How Christians are to live in the light of their salvation. His pastoral care centers around focusing on Christ. Knowing God will shape our hearts and help in our progress towards the final day.

It *seems* simple – Keep your eyes fixed on Jesus, stay on course, read your Bible and pray…

So, if it's that simple, why does it actually feel so hard?

There are things that slow us down. There are times in our lives when we just feel a bit "meh". We get in our own way when we compare ourselves to others. Sometimes we feel like this "journey" is just taking forever and frankly, we're tired. It's during these times that we feel like losers.

Things that slow you down

Let me paint you a picture. Brand new boats start out with slick and shiny hulls, but gradually their hulls become home to algae and barnacles. So soon, instead of slicing through the waves like a hot knife through butter, you're thumping through the water like a pig on a trampoline. It happens gradually though, so you might not necessarily realise it's happening. But over time, there is a definite and seemingly unstoppable build up of gunk that slows you down. All boats have to have their hulls cleaned.

And life's a lot like that. There are all manner of things that build up on us as we go through life – overwork, anxiety, money worries, difficult relationships, the pressure of our culture, social media, and parenting stress to name a few. There are an unlimited number of things that cumulatively (and individually) inhibit our ability to move through life. When we are constantly encumbered like that, it feels like *everything* is a barnacle slowing us down – including our faith. We can deal with one thing at a time to try and address things, but in the end, we just need to be pulled out of the water and have all those accretions chipped off, and the hull given a good scrubbing.

Hebrews 12:1 says *"Therefore, since we are surrounded by such a great cloud of witnesses,* **let us throw off everything that hinders and the sin that so easily entangles.** *And let us run with perseverance the race marked out for us"* (my emphasis). We've just got to get in there and get rid of these things. It sounds easy. It's not. But that's what the Bible tells us we've got to do.

When you feel a bit "meh"

Here are some more good metaphors: All relationships go stale. All journeys become tiresome. All projects get a bit boring. All fires die down. Things start off strong and then just meander along, and before we know it, things have become a bit…blah.

We feel it deep within us. It can be a nagging feeling at the back of our minds or in the pit of our stomachs. We know we're becoming lukewarm. We don't feel the fire anymore: our prayers have become formulaic; our personal devotions are not that personal and not really devoted; our church going has become just something we "do". Worse, going to church feels like a chore, or we go to church searching for how it was in the beginning, and come away unsatisfied.

We feel guilty because we're not "bringing it" and feeling things madly all the time. We feel adrift because we don't really belong in "church world" and we don't really belong in the real world. We feel embarrassed because everyone around us just seems to be so godly and so faithful and so committed and frankly, so *good* at being Christian. So we put our church faces on and hope we don't get found out.

"I know your deeds, that you are neither cold nor hot. I wish you were either one or the other! So, because you are lukewarm—neither hot nor cold—I am about to spit you out of my mouth." (Revelation 3:15-16)

These are John's prophetic words in Revelation and this passage is from the letter to the church in Laodicea. John wrote these words to a church in western Turkey nearly two thousand years ago. But I think we can all recognize there is wisdom in here for us too. In all honesty, these words make me feel uncomfortable. But the great thing is when we keep reading, we are told what to do about this state of affairs. In verses 19-20 it says:

"Those whom I love I rebuke and discipline. So be earnest and repent. Here I am! I stand at the door and knock. If anyone hears my voice and opens the door, I will come in and eat with that person, and they with me."

It recognizes that people are lukewarm, but there is a way to change things. The worst thing we can do is pretend that lukewarm is okay and keep on going the way we are.

This kind of "okay" means the fire goes cold.

This kind of "okay" means the relationship gradually dies.

So what is the answer?

It might help to think of the Christian life as a race which is how Paul describes it. In 2 Timothy 4:7 Paul says he has finished the race and kept the faith. A race takes effort. Running takes effort. I hate running. When I run, bits of me jiggle that really shouldn't. Running is boring and difficult.

But if the New Testament tells us that the Christian life is like a race, we have to do something. We can't ignore it. If it's a race, we can't go onto cruise control. We have to go at a certain speed. We have to stay alert. We have to plan and strategize about how to get to the finish. We have to be able to move and adapt as circumstances change. Being lukewarm is one of those times.

When we compare ourselves to others

Sometimes (okay, a lot of the time) I compare myself to others who seem to have it all "together". I also compare myself to this mythical perfect Christian – the one who can, and is, doing all the things that I think I should be doing. Where did we get this mythical creature? Where did we get this list of do's and don'ts? They aren't written down anywhere, like they're a new "10 commandments of Christian living". They are things we all recognize though:

- Read your Bible every day
- Pray every day
- Put church above all else
- Only take in what is edifying
- Commit fully to a community of believers
- Evangelize others

- Pastorally care for others
- Keep your eyes fixed on Jesus

This list makes sense. They are wise activities for the faithful because if we want to be obedient and grow in Christlikeness, these are the kinds of things we need to work on and seek the Spirit's help to develop.

I see people who I think are doing all the things on this list and I have the impression that they are bundles of relentless energy. I assume that 100% of their lives are focused on God's kingdom and their focus never wavers. I feel that if I was to be 100% focused, I would have to live in a convent or a retreat and never speak to another human. But that rather defeats the purpose.

So how are we to work on these expressions of Christian living, bearing in mind that these are expressions of where our saved heart wants to be?

When the journey drags on

The metaphor I've gone with for this book is a journey – because the Christian life is the journey of a lifetime. It's a helpful metaphor because most, if not all, of us have been stuck in a car on a long journey that seems interminable. No doubt it started off strong. We have our clothes neatly packed in the suitcase, we have all our travel documents checked and re-checked and organized. We are excited and a little bit scared, but the anticipation drives us forward and we're dying to get cracking.

After a while, travelling gets a bit messy. Those documents are wallowing at the bottom of your bag somewhere and your suitcase has become a lucky dip of dirty socks and undies. You're tired of travelling, it's inconvenient. The car is covered in mud and the handbrake is sticking. The scenery becomes a bit boring and your travelling companions are annoying. And many of us know the cold feeling of irritation that rises through our shoulders and neck as we hear a little person say, "Are we there yet?"

No. We are not there yet. And we have a long way to go. The plea of the little person is echoed in your own brain. This journey is taking *for-ever*!!

Telling a weary traveler to keep their eyes fixed on the destination is good advice but it doesn't take away from the grating toil of the journey itself. Telling someone to read the map every day is also good advice but what if you're rubbish at reading maps? Then you start getting stressed and confused and the journey becomes a special kind of torture. What if reading the map makes you car sick? Alright, this is where the metaphor breaks down, but you get the idea. Just doing what seems straight forward is not as clear and as easy as it seems.

But it is important on our journey that we are not passive observers. We can't sink down in our seats and stare blankly out of the window.

Think of this book firstly as a pit-stop. This is where you get to pull off the road, get a cuppa, stretch your legs and re-group before carrying on. Secondly, think of it as an opportunity to get your bearings once again. To remember where you're going and why. By the time you get back in the car, you're raring to go again.

The aim of this book is to help you continue with your Christian journey in the midst of your normal, sometimes messy, life. The Bible is full of amazing wisdom to help us persevere on our Christian journey. So in each Chapter we will be gathering the treasure of Scripture to help spur us forward.

We'll start by looking at our identity in Christ and our citizenship in heaven as a foundational reminder that our salvation has already happened.

Then, each chapter will start with a proposition of what we think we should be doing or thinking, based on our list of do's and don'ts – it will present the ideal picture of where we think we should be and the reality of where we often find ourselves.

We'll explore the reality and the disjoint between the reality and the ideal. And then we'll head to the Bible to drill down on its practical, specific and realistic wisdom to find an answer to the question of how to keep going as Christians in the midst of our messy lives .

Always remember though, you have been saved by God's grace through Jesus' sacrifice on the cross. That is not in question here. I would hate for you to read this book and think you need to add another thing to a list of do's and don'ts. We are not saved by things that we do. We have been saved by Jesus.

What we are talking about here is all the stuff that comes after that, while we live in our broken world, in our messy lives. How do we stay focused? How do we stay obedient?

We can't live perfect lives. Only Jesus did that. But, with God's help, we can stand firm and continue to grow in faith. As Paul told the Philippians:

"In all my prayers for all of you, I always pray with joy because of your partnership in the gospel from the first day until now, being confident of this, that he who began a good work in you will carry it on to completion until the day of Christ Jesus." (Philippians 1:4-6)

God saved us through Jesus' blood and now sanctifies us through the Spirit to make us worthy of our calling. God does this work. But we are willing partners. This book is about what *we* can do to keep our stamina and keep each other going on this journey of a lifetime.

Chapter 2
Remember Who You Are

What I think I should think:
I am a child of God

What I generally think:
I have so many hats I don't know who I am anymore

Identity is a big deal. Knowing who we are and what we believe about ourselves, underpins what we do, why and how.

We hear in church all the time about our new identity in Christ and like so many things, we can hear the words, and understand them and marvel at them – and yet not necessarily accept them about ourselves personally. We can know what Christ did for us and yet still believe the most humdrum parts of our life define us as a person. We can have immense faith in Christ, but little faith in ourselves. This corrosive self-belief makes our approach to the list of do's and don'ts problematic.

In this chapter we're going to work through what we think our identity is and then map that against what the Bible says it is. What we'll also look at is the gap between the two – and how to bridge it. Then we can think through the rest of our discipleship on a foundation of solid identity in Christ rather than identity in ourselves.

Who do you think you are?

Identity seems like a more complicated concept than it actually is.

Identity is the concept we develop about ourselves. It's how we make sense of ourselves. It's what it means to be *you*. This develops and evolves over time. We inherit some of our identity – we internalize values from our parents and our culture – but eventually, we form our own. We develop as our authentic selves. The real us, with our own values and views.

In some ways, identity exists in real time, as in, it's who you are right now. In other ways it's aspirational, it's who you would like to be in the future. The person you are working towards being.

So let's do a bit of a thought experiment.

In the olden days people wore hats. This had long been the case but was particularly so during the Industrial Revolution when there was a massive increase in new and different occupations and specializations. This was the era that the term "to wear many hats" was first used. Different roles, functions and occupations could be identified by one's hat. The butcher, the baker, the cook, the miner, the teacher, the lawyer, all wore different head-gear. So, the saying goes, if one wears many hats, then one has many roles or occupations. Back then, it was something so out of the ordinary that it required a special phrase to describe it. Today, it's the norm.

What are your hats? Write them down if it helps. Put a star next to the ones that you think are the most important to you. Here are some of mine by way of example:

1. A parent and therefore also a:
    a. Chef
    b. Nurse
    c. Teacher

    d. Judge and arbiter
    e. Engineer
    f. Counselor
    g. Chauffeur
    h. Dental hygienist
    i. Laundress
    j. Peace keeping force
2. Employee
3. Friend
4. Christian
5. Bible study leader
6. Daughter
7. Housekeeper.

And these are just the ones I can think of off the top of my head.

And these roles change. Over time, new hats are required, old hats fall out of use. Sometimes the transition takes place gradually. At other times, the change is a rude shock. When that happens, we are all faced with that uncertainty – "Who am I?" Or, at times of despair or loss we might cry inwardly "Is this all I am? Is this all there is?"

People feel this to different degrees, men and women, young and old from all over the world, and it's as profound and devastating to everyone, in all their unique circumstances.

How then, when we have so much required of us in the here-and-now, do we pause enough to remember we are a child of God? What does that even mean? And what does it have to do with what I have to do *right now*?

This is so important for us on this journey. Because there are so many things that can pull us off course. And losing our sense of self can take us right off track. Losing our sense of identity means we can find ourselves drawing our identity from things that are not necessarily healthy. At worst, we can become so busy and blind, that our many "hats" cover up the one "hat" that is most important.

Given that we've just had a quick think about our hats and which are most important to us, how then do we pin down what our identity is? Have a think about some of these things:

- What are your strengths? (e.g. I am a good friend, I am a hard worker etc.)
- What are your passions?
- What are your values and what do you think is your core or highest prized value?
- What is important to you? (A good way to test this is to think about what you would do if you only had 4 weeks left on earth? If you suddenly had $1 million, what would you spend it on? If you had an extra room in your house, what would you use it for?)
- What do you want your epitaph to be?
- How do you express your identity in ways that you want others to perceive it? (For example, in how you dress, what you drive, what you post on social media, what clubs and groups you are a member of?)

The answers to these questions will give you a window into how you see yourself and how that affects your day to day decisions, attitudes and behaviors. Being aware of this is a really powerful tool in being able to see what is real and authentic in our daily lives – but this awareness might also show us where we need God to help shape us.

Who does the Bible say you are?

The Bible has a lot to say about who we are. In 2 Thessalonians 2:13-17, Paul says:

"But we ought always to thank God for you, **brothers and sisters loved** by the Lord, because God **chose** you as **firstfruits** to be saved through the sanctifying work of the Spirit and through belief in the truth. He **called** you to this through our gospel, that you might **share** in the glory of our Lord Jesus Christ.

So then, brothers and sisters, stand firm and hold fast to the teachings we passed on to you, whether by word of mouth or by letter.

May our Lord Jesus Christ himself and God our **Father**, who loved us and by his grace gave us eternal encouragement and good **hope**, encourage your hearts and strengthen you in every good deed and word."

There are several descriptors in these verses that apply to all of us as believers which should, and does, inform our identity in Christ.

We are family

It was translated as "brothers" in the old Bible and amended to "brothers and sisters" in the new modern NIV translation to be inclusive. The Greek word is *adelphoi* and does mean brothers in the strictest sense. However, in addressing a crowd, the plural masculine was used in a gender-neutral sense to address both men and women. As *adelphoi* we are all related. We are family. This is part of our identity in Christ – the fact that we are connected to others in a very real and profound sense.

We are loved

This phrase can seem so obvious that it's tempting to pass it over. Of course we know we are loved. But do we? Do we really? Sometimes it can be hard to believe or even accept. But we are. Say it to yourself and know it. I am loved by God.

We are chosen

I find this mind blowing. We are chosen by God. Not for anything we have done or are going to do. We were chosen long before we were born to be with God in heaven for all eternity.

We are the first fruits

First fruits relate to the first produce of an agricultural season, typically offered to God. In Deuteronomy, God tells his people that when they enter the promised land they are to gather some of the first fruits and offer them to him with a mark of remembrance of how he saved them from Egypt and brought them to Canaan. Then they are to rejoice at all that God has done (Deuteronomy 26:1-11). In 2 Thessalonians, Paul describes us as the first fruits. If we are the first fruits, we are the first crop of a new season and we are to be offered to God. This means our whole selves are a mark of remembrance and rejoicing. It's worth stopping to think how that flows through into our lives if this is a part of our identity in Christ.

We are called

You might find this a little challenging. The idea of being called by God might make you feel intimidated, or nervous at the weight of what it might mean. Either because you don't feel good enough, or because you don't feel ready and equipped enough. Here are some things to remember though. First, God called all manner of people who on the surface of things, seem entirely inappropriate. But he called them and preserved them and upheld them. Moses, who was a murderer, is a prime example here (Exodus 2:11-15). Rahab was a prostitute (Joshua 2:1), and Ruth was a foreigner (Ruth 2:10).

Second, God didn't call people who were ready to pick up whatever challenge lay ahead. He called people and then gave them all the training and skills they needed. Again, Moses is a prime example. And Elisha was called and trained by Elijah before he took over his prophetic ministry.

Third, we're not all called to be Moses or Elijah or even Rahab or Ruth. We don't know what we're called to do in God's great plan. But we know we're called to be faithful. That might entail something mighty, or it might involve tiny acts of obedience that have a ripple effect far beyond what is seen.

Fourth, we are reassured with the reminder that we are supposed to be jars of clay:

"*But we have this treasure in jars of clay to show that this all-surpassing power is from God and not from us.*" (2 Corinthians 4:7)

We are not supposed to be perfect – that is for God alone. We are meant to be the vulnerable and broken people that we are. But we can still, if we remain faithful and obedient, achieve what God has purposed for us to do, whether that be raising our kids, bringing Christian behaviour to a secular workplace, witnessing to our friends, running a ministry or going on mission.

Fifth, and finally, we were called by *God*. That is huge. Who is God that he is mindful of us? Perhaps the alternate is easier for us to grasp – as it says in Psalm 8, verse 4, "*what is mankind that you are mindful of them, human beings that you care for them?*" Just as Ruth had said to Boaz, her kinsman redeemer in Ruth 2:10 when she asked, "*why have I found such favor in your eyes that you notice me – a foreigner?*" We have done nothing. The truth that we are called by God is not about us, it is about God and his will and purposes. In Isaiah 43:7, the prophet tells us that God created everyone who calls on his name for his glory (not ours). And, since we are just foreigners and outsiders, it is amazing that God, the creator of the universe, made us and wants us.

What a wonderful and beautiful thing, to be called by God himself.

We share in Christ's glory

In the gospel of John, when he talks about Christ's glorification, John is talking about Jesus' crucifixion, not his resurrection or ascension. The cross is Christ's glory. How are we to share in that?

"*I have been crucified with Christ and I no longer live, but Christ lives in me. The life I now live in the body, I live by faith in the Son of God, who loved me and gave himself for me."* (Galatians 2:20) We were crucified with Christ. The crucifixion was the moment that united the whole universe. In that moment all our sins were paid for. We share in this moment with Jesus. We are united to him in this moment.

God is our Father

I sometimes have a hard time getting my head around this. God is my *Father*. So while I appreciate his raw power and sovereignty, I can trust him and go to him because he knows me better than I know myself. I couldn't hide anything from him even if I wanted to. I am so small. An ant. And yet his Father-ship makes me significant.

We have hope

We have hope in heaven, but we also have a sure hope in God and his promises and his sovereignty and his providence. We can trust him. This gives us an optimism. Because no matter how bad things get, God is with us.

So now, along with your own list of self-identifying elements, here's a list of what we are told in 2 Thessalonians:

- I have a new family;
- I am loved;
- I am chosen;
- I am part of God's first-fruits;
- I am called;
- I share in God's glory;
- God is my Father;
- I have hope.

Map your "Who do you think you are" points against what the Bible says about your identity. Can you map one against the other? Do you see trends or differences or gaps?

Bridging the gap

We will all see trends, differences or gaps – and though it might be tempting to see these areas as deficiencies that's not the goal. This exercise is merely designed to expose how close we feel ourselves to finding our identity in Christ. It is meant to be a fact-finding exercise: that is, to expose the facts of the case. There is no judgement involved, it's just being able to recognise how things are right now.

In many ways it doesn't matter if you don't feel like a child of God, the point is **you already are.** You might have trouble feeling confidence in the title "child of the king". That's okay. Your status before God and your identity in Christ does not depend on your confidence. It depends on God. So even when we are at our weakest and most lost moments, our status stays strong and true. We are weak, but he is strong.

So, if this is our identity already, how does that mesh with our present self?

It means for starters that there is a hat we wear all the time… a hat that we never have to change… a hat that reveals who we are that can never be taken from us. Whether you feel good or bad, confident or fragile, you are a child of God.

You may need to get to know yourself in light of this reminder. That won't mean seeking counselling, or adventures that push you to the limits, or cloistering yourself away in silence for weeks in order to discover your true identity. We just need to get to know ourselves and appreciate ourselves in the light of what God knows about us.

An interesting exercise is to read 1 Corinthians 13:4-7 but change the word "love" to "I". It refocusses us on how we should be in our identity. Bear in mind, we can't nail all this all the time so don't be downhearted! It's merely a useful tool to slow us down and refocus on our eternal identity. This is a statement of acknowledgement of what we want to be in Christ. Read it aloud and pray under God for the Spirit to help you fulfill your God given identity.

"I am patient, I am kind. I do not envy, I do not boast, I am not proud. I do not dishonor others, I am not self-seeking, I am not easily angered, I keep no record of wrongs. I do not delight in evil but rejoice with the truth. I always protect, always trust, always hope, always persevere."

Explore your identity in Christ. Grow your confidence in this identity and work out how it is expressed outwardly in your life.

Some 'hats' might continue to be important to you. Some 'hats' might be no longer necessary. You will find yourself changing as you reflect on who you are and what being a child of God looks like. Remember though – this is a process, a journey. It doesn't happen all at once.

I love this quote from C. S. Lewis from *Mere Christianity:* "The more we get what we now call "ourselves" out of the way and let Him take us over, the more truly ourselves we become... It is no good trying to "be myself" without Him. The more I resist Him and try to live on my own, the more I become dominated by my own heredity and upbringing and surroundings and natural desires... I am not, in my natural state, nearly so much of a person as I like to believe: most of what I call "me" can be very easily explained. It is when I turn to Christ, when I give myself up to His Personality, that I first begin to have a real personality of my own." (*Mere Christianity*)

Remember also this: "And I am sure of this, that he who began a good work in you will bring it to completion at the day of Jesus Christ." (Philippians 1:6) This process was begun in us by Him, and He will complete it. We are not just passengers though. How we live this out in day-to-day life is something we get to make choices about. If we can continue on this journey being confident in our identity in him, this is the most important foundation we can lay.

Chapter 3
Fake it til you make it

What I think I should be doing:
I will read my Bible every day

What generally happens:
Time just gets away from me

The Proposition

"The Proposition" is that we should read our Bibles every day. I can hear your heart sinking already – don't worry, this isn't a super short chapter just saying "read your Bible". Like I said, if it was that easy, we'd all be doing it.

I think we'd all love to be the person who reads our Bible every day, but life just seems to get in the way. So, is the Proposition a good goal?

Eighteenth-century pastor and founder of the Methodist movement John Wesley said, *"I am a creature of a day. I am a spirit come from God, and returning to God. I want to know one thing: the way to heaven. God himself has condescended to teach me the way. He has written it down in a book."* If we are to know God and if we are to know where we are heading, we need to know God's communication to us.

But daily? Alrighty, let's be clear – reading the Bible isn't like a test or homework that's going to get graded. We're not terrible Christians if we don't read it every day. But it's *wise* to engage with God's word as often as possible, and daily is a good habit. Why? We need to make sure our minds are alert (1 Peter 1:13). I don't know about you, but I need daily mental preparation. I can't keep myself on course for longer than a day (or an hour) so the *frequency* and *regularity* of Bible reading is really important.

What does regularly engaging with the Bible do?

Proverbs 5:21 says, *"For your ways are in full view of the Lord, and he examines all your paths."* God knows us and sees everything. He knows us better than we know ourselves. We do not know ourselves as well as we think we do. Our brains do things that we are not at all aware of. Our emotions trick us. Our thoughts betray us. We are foggy at best.

It's the difference between light and darkness:

> *"The path of the righteous is like the morning sun,*
> *shining ever brighter till the full light of day.*
> *But the way of the wicked is like deep darkness;*
> *they do not know what makes them stumble."*
> (Proverbs 4:18-19)

There's a two-tone feeling in verse 18. There's the light of the morning sun, lighting the way of believers as we walk. Then there's the full light of day, the high point we are aiming for. Whereas the wicked don't even know what is making them stumble, let alone have enough light to see the end goal.

The Israelites themselves lost the Scriptures. Yes, actually lost them! 2 Kings 22:8-23:3 described Josiah, King of Judah, refurbishing the temple in Jerusalem. This was about 640 years before the birth of Christ and about 300 years after King Solomon. So within 300 years, God's word had been forgotten so completely that The Book of the Law[1] when found and read, caused enormous shock and (thankfully) repentance and revival in Judah.

For us, that would be like forgetting, and re-discovering, *Gulliver's Travels* or the American Declaration of Independence. Except this was the book of God's law – a document of exceptional significance and social and spiritual importance. It meant that for 300 years, the Israelites had been going off track. It meant that God was remembered only vaguely as a shadow or a memory. How could they possibly know what God wanted of them and for them?

The *entire* Book of the Law was supposed to have been read to the Israelites every seven years (Deuteronomy 31:10-13) so the people could listen and learn to fear God and walk in His ways. This suggests to me that listening, learning, fearing and walking the way we are supposed to needs consistent support. Every seven years was specific reading of the book of the Law from the elders, but Proverbs and the Psalms, particularly Psalm 119, shows that meditation on God's work is a regular and constant pre-occupation. There are wonderful things in God's law (Psalm 119:18), the psalmist's soul is consumed with longing for God's laws at all times (v20), there is delight in God's words (v47) and comfort (v50) and hope (v14).

Your word is a lamp for my feet and a light on my path, says the psalmist (v105), and his flesh trembles in fear of God (v120), but there is salvation in God's words (v123).

Salvation. God's words contain salvation. Not just end-goal salvation, but daily support so we don't fall away like the people who lost The Book of the Law. Because that's how easy it is to forget.

---

[1] That is the Pentateuch, or the first five books of the Bible as we know it.

"See to it, brothers and sisters, that none of you has a sinful, unbelieving heart that turns away from the living God. But encourage one another daily, as long as it is called "Today," so that none of you may be hardened by sin's deceitfulness." (Hebrews 3:12-13)

Jesus himself said that whoever wanted to be his disciple must take up their cross daily (Luke 9:23). *Daily*. God knows us so well. He knows how quickly we forget. We need to re-calibrate every day. The effects of regular Bible engagement can also be empirically measured[2]. Regular Bible engagement (in the case of this study, that is four or more times a week), decreased temptations to various desires significantly. Temptations to drink to excess, view pornography, gamble, lash out in anger, gossip, and overeat/mishandle food or money decreased by up to 62%. Struggles with feelings of bitterness, self-destructive thoughts or thoughts about others and difficulty with forgiveness decreased by up to 40%. Participants had a significantly increased personal proactive faith and greatly reduced feelings of being spiritually stagnant or feeling like they can't please God.

It's not really surprising that engaging with God more often produces positive effects and reduces negative effects. Engaging with God's word *actually works*. And remembering and re-remembering that it works can help you keep engaging with God's word.

Why can't I read my Bible every day?

I have a big problem. I know I need to go to the gym. I know it will be good for me. All the research, the doctors and the empirical evidence tells me that exercising will prolong my life and generally do lots of good

---

[2] Arnold Cole & Pamela Caudill Ovwigho, *Bible Engagement as the Key to Spiritual Growth: A Research Synthesis* (Centre of Bible Engagement, www.c4be.org August 2012).

things for my health and wellbeing. But I'd still rather stay here on the couch and eat Cheezels.

One of the things I dislike more than going to the gym is being *told* I should go to the gym. The people who tell me this are well meaning, good intentioned people. They are also super fit and gorgeous which does not make me inclined to acquiesce.

The point is I *know* I should do it. But I still don't. I could be lazy. That may well be true (and probably is) but it's an overly simplistic view of something that is far more nuanced. We need to break down the "Why" in two ways. First, what are my human barriers, that I am aware of? And second, what is my brain and body doing that hinders me, that I'm not even aware of?

What are my human barriers?

This is where I drill down on why I don't like going to the gym:

1. It's physically difficult
2. I don't like getting changed – I get cold and it's a hassle
3. I don't like getting sweaty – I find it gross and uncomfortable
4. It makes me feel unattractive and embarrassed

Each of these items can be drilled down on further and overcome, but for now, it's worth noting that "being lazy" is not a hugely helpful assessment of the situation. It would be a bit mean of someone to say it to me; and saying it to myself puts a downward pressure on my motivation and my self-esteem.

It's far more helpful to think more about the Why in the more practical terms I've outlined above. When we get more picky, more critical in our self-analysis, it helps us to work out what's really going on.

They might be good reasons. They might be bad reasons. But they'll be your honest and realistic assessment of your barriers.

How does my brain hinder me?

Now let's talk about Hyperbolic Discounting and Decision Fatigue. Sound snazzy don't they? Please don't be put off. These are just two terms that important clever-type people came up with to describe things that happen in all our brains.

Hyperbolic Discounting describes how the human brain will choose small rewards sooner, rather than wait for a larger reward. It's linked closely to dopamine which is a neuro-transmitter controlling the reward areas of the brain. So, here's what happens – I see or think about a reward (this would include weighing up whether I go to the gym for the long-term reward of being fitter or stay here on the couch with my short-term Cheezel reward). My brain will seize on the short-term reward and the dopamine areas of my brain will light up like a Christmas tree. That's because dopamine is part of a primal response mechanism that tells the brain what is important for its survival right now. That's why it likes short-term rewards. The idea of long-term rewards doesn't result in the same flood of dopamine because a longer term goal is less important to our immediate survival.

What does this mean? It means that our brains will automatically go for the Cheezels every time. Even though we know the gym is the better option, our dopamine levels have already triggered what our response will be. And that's because dopamine also communicates with the rest of our body. The dopamine doesn't just send signals about what to choose, it controls our movement so we actually go about achieving those goals. So even though intellectually I know what the better option is, by the time I have even finished thinking the thought, my capacious behind is already aimed with ill-advised speed at the couch.

Can we trick our brains? Or out-think them? We can. However, before we get to that, we need to briefly look at Decision Fatigue. Because this is the other key way that our own brains hinder us.

Decision Fatigue is exactly what it sounds like – it's when we get mentally tired of having to make choices. Our brains are making choices all the time, even when we are not conscious of it. What scientists are finding now is that we have a finite amount of will-power every day. It only replenishes after sleep (i.e. when our brains are switched off for a while). That's why our will-power and decision-making ability is strongest in the morning and diminishes during the day.

So again, we can see that our motivation is not "lacking" as such (we're not just "lazy"). There are other things at play that we need to consider. There are things we are not even aware of happening, that are critical factors affecting our motivation.

How motives and motivation affect decision making

Motives and motivation are not the same thing. Motives are our reasons. My reason for going to the gym is to get healthy. Motivation however is something else entirely and can be affected by all manner of external and internal factors.

Motivation can be strong or weak based on the need or desire for an object and the intensity of the need or desire. The intensity can be driven by how important the object is to us personally. For instance, does it feed into our sense of identity (which is important), or just a feeling that it's something I should do (which is potentially not so important to us).

Motivation intensity can be affected by incentives and the stimulus to fulfill goals.

What this all means is that cumulatively, a lot of factors can negatively or positively affect our decision to "go to the gym". And okay, by now you will have worked out that when I say "go to the gym" I am really talking about "doing my personal devotions". Please don't switch off at this point! Hopefully what you've seen by now is that saying "just read your Bible and pray" is about as useful as saying "go to the gym". It's true, but there is a lot more involved.

But let's stop for a minute – "devotions" is a pretty old-fashioned word these days so what do I mean when I say "doing my personal devotions"?

In Acts 1:14 the disciples are described as being joined together constantly in prayer and, again, in Acts 2:42 the disciples were continually devoted to the apostles teaching. The word for constantly/continually devoted is the same in both verses. It is προσκαρτερέω (*proskartereó*) which goes further than just "constantly". It means to keep doing something assiduously (as it's used in 1:14), and with perseverance, perhaps even despite obstacles (when it's used in 2:42). Either way, there is certainly *effort* implied.

Devotion was, and is, involved with reading God's word, thinking about it, meditating on it, and praying, making an effort to do it. And doing it a lot.

What was the disciples' motive? What was their motivation? It is important to note that just prior to Acts 1:14 the disciples had seen Jesus ascend into heaven and just prior to 2:42, Pentecost had happened. That's quite strong motivation. They had seen the risen Christ, they had experienced his power and everything was slotting into place based on what he had taught them prior to the crucifixion. It was clear, it was immediate, it was mind expanding. They approached the Scriptures with a renewed vigor, knowing that each time they would learn something new about who Jesus was and what he had come to do. They were hungry and they were expectant.

Jesus often sought solitude to pray (it's worth reading Mark 1:35, Luke 6:12-13, Matthew 14:13 and 23 and Luke 9:18). It's too long a bow to call these "devotions" in our modern sense of the word, but what it shows is Jesus himself removing himself from whatever is happening, to spend time communicating with God the Father. This was clearly an important element to his relationship with God. We'll look at prayer in a later chapter, but here it is important to note the behavior and setting. Jesus takes deliberate time. He removes himself from whatever is happening. He finds solitude to be alone with God. These are critical elements we should bring to our own "devotions". We should take care not to be hurried or distracted. We should make time for them and find a place where we can keep our focus as we do them.

Devoted to Devotions

Engaging with God on a personal level is not a new or modern idea, although historically it hasn't been an easy thing to achieve. Before a few hundred years ago, there were no available Bibles believers could access or read. Only people who entered monasteries or convents could spend this kind of precious time in hearing and meditating on God's words and even then, it was highly structured and all in Latin. Making Bibles available to believers in their own language so they could read God's words for themselves became a labour of love for the growing reforming movement in the sixteenth century and was hard fought for.

William Tyndale was a mild-mannered but focused cleric and academic intent on translating the Bible into English and making it accessible to everyone. His reforming tendencies drove him into exile on the Continent where he published his English Bible in 1526. Nine years later he was captured and executed.

He once asked *"Do you know who taught the eagles to find their prey? Well, that same God teaches His hungry children to find their Father in His Word."*

Tyndale wasn't the only one to suffer for bringing the Bible to the people. People still suffer for it today. We are incredibly blessed in the

West to have safe and easy access to the Bible. For us, it is literally a click or a swipe away.

While the Reformation paved the way for people to access and read the Bible and know God for themselves, a group called "The Pietists" developed a deeper and richer idea of personal piety and how to live out a Christian life. Their ways of Bible reading, meditation and prayer would be more what we understand as "devotions" or "quiet time". The Pietists brought their influence to both America and England, the latter particularly via John Wesley.

John Wesley was the founder of the Methodist movement in the mid-18th century. It was through this revival that personal piety became encouraged, enhanced and organized. If we were to travel in time and see one of Wesley's organized weekly meetings, it would look very much to us like a weekly Growth Group or Connect Group, except probably with a lot less snacks. There were conditions of membership set out in three General Rules drawn up in 1743 and under rule number three, taking part in family and private prayer, and searching of the Scriptures are key requirements.

Throughout history, there have been key figures who modelled and taught that regular engagement with God is pivotal to knowing God for *ourselves*.

Taking Control of Your Bible Reading

The big picture is this: we are to love the Lord our God with all of our minds and hearts and souls. How are we to do that if we don't engage with Him? If I don't engage with God through word, meditation and prayer, every day, I am increasing my chances of falling away and increasing the likelihood that my daily life will not be guided by God in obedience and discernment. It decreases my chances of living my life in a way that is most glorifying to God and most joyful for me.

It *does not* mean I am lazy. It *does* mean that there are factors at play that I need to recognize and deal with, to the best of my ability and with God's help. So, if you're like me and struggle with daily engagement with God, here are some things we can think about and try.

1. Write a list and critically analyze what it is about engagement time that you don't like or that stops you from doing it. Looking at the list in black and white might help us to overcome the obstacles we've identified. The less easy ones are ones we can bring before God in prayer.
2. Be mindful of Hyperbolic Discounting – make short-term goals. Perhaps a Bible study focused on the shorter letters or books of the Bible or a devotional that has a short-term end. There are lots of apps that offer Bible reading programs that last for 3, 5 or 7 days.
3. Be aware of Decision Fatigue. Try to remove having to make choices – for example, have a set time and a set place to read the Bible so you don't even have to think about it. If you need additional incentive, meet up with someone at a set time and place – like having a gym buddy. This helps with that tricky dopamine issue and weighing up a short-term goal and a longer-term benefit. Avoiding decision making avoids a short-term goal takeover in the brain.
4. The disciples were continually devoted because they had met the risen Jesus. In essence, so have we. If it seems shadowy, have a look at the chapter on "Going in for a Service" to help re-remember the love you had at first.
5. We can help our motivation by having a big mission and an incentive plan. I don't mean we're allowed a Mars bar when we finish each book of the Bible (although...). What I do mean is tying God's mission to our own heart's desires. Ultimately,

I want to stand before God and hear Him tell me I have been a good and faithful servant. I long for it more than I can say. It speaks to my identity. It speaks to my most intense desire. What's yours? Meditate on that, and when you find it, write it down so you can keep going back to it. Under that then, you can map out what incentives fit with your personal mission.

6. Remember God wants this for us. It's not a test. His word is a lamp for our feet. He doesn't want us to stumble, He wants us with Him. He knows our struggle. Lean on Him, ask Him for help, just like the Psalmist did. Read through Psalm 119, a chunk at a time (it's really long) and think about it, and pray about it.

So, if the Proposition is a reasonable goal, how do we balance that with the reality of our lives? My first thought when I'm told something like "read your Bible daily" is "That's easy for you to say." And that's a perfectly reasonable response. So, let's look at this in a completely different way...

Remember Grace

Here's something we haven't talked about – it's okay to not know how to do it. In the sections above, we've talked about there being the *will*, but we haven't talked about the *way*. There are lots of apps and devotional books to help you but don't be afraid to ask around to find out how other people do their engagement time. It's always good to have a range of ideas to try for yourself.

Secondly, sometimes you just have to fake it till you make it. Engaging with God through his word is not a suggestion for us, it's not just a "nice to do, it's a "critical to do". If we aren't engaging with Him, something may be wrong with our relationship. God is bringing 100%.

He always has and He always will. So we need to work on our end. If we wait until we are ready and all the circumstances are right, we might never do it. Sometimes, you just need to start a habit to get going.

It is not always easy though. So lastly, never give up trying. If you try one thing and you can't stick at it, prayerfully try it again. If it's still not working for you, try something else. You might be in a stage where things are incredibly difficult – new parenthood, a poor emotional state, a situation adversely affecting your mental health. Lots of things can affect our capacity to engage with God's word. Please remember that reading the Bible is not the benchmark for your Christian life.

Please remember that other people are struggling too, even though they might look as though they have it all together.

Please remember that reading the Bible is not about "looking Christian", it's about feeding your heart with God's precious words.

This is where it all starts. If we don't go to the gym, we'll probably get a bit soft around the middle and our fitness will suffer. If we don't engage with God, the risks are so much greater. So please remember to never give up trying.

The Christian journey is the journey of a lifetime. Everything begins and ends with God, and Jesus who is the image of the invisible God. The place we get to know Jesus is in the Bible. And if we know Jesus, we know God. The Bible is where we meet the risen Christ. It's where we hear God's voice. It teaches us how to pray and how to engage with God. The more we do it, the higher the likelihood of approaching God hungry and expectant. The more we do it, the closer we'll get to constant devotion. It will replenish our stamina for the journey.

The more stamina we have, the easier the journey gets and the brighter the view out of the windows.

Chapter 4
ACTS and Teaspoons

What I think I should be doing:
Praying about everything all the time

What generally happens
My prayer life is a bit hit and miss

The Proposition

The Proposition here is that prayer should be the first thing we do each day, and the thing we do consistently, frequently and perfectly throughout the rest of the day. I say "perfectly" because we often feel like there is "a way" to pray and whatever "the way" is, we're not doing it.

Before we go on, let's ditch the idea that prayer has to be perfect in any way, because intellectually, I think we all know that that's not possible or reasonable. We can follow ACTS prayers (Adoration, Confession, Thanksgiving, Supplication) and Teaspoon prayers (TSP – Thank you, Sorry and Please) to give ourselves a formula to go by, which is why, funnily enough, prayer can seem so formulaic.

But is the rest of the Proposition reasonable? The Bible tells us often that prayer should be first and foremost in our behavior. So, here, we'll look at what the Bible tells us prayer is for, and then we'll focus on the gap between what we think we should be doing, and what we are really doing.

What is prayer actually for?

The first clear time that prayer is mentioned in the Bible is Genesis 4:26 when, after the Fall and lots of "knowing" and "begetting", the people started to call on the name of the Lord. We can't tell what form or content this took but it's clear this happened after people were separated from God and wanted to acknowledge him and ask for his blessing somehow.

So, prayer is something that can connect us with God, even though we are separated.

How do long distance relationships work? If you Google "How to make long distance relationships work" there are some common threads that are bizarrely helpful. Staying in contact is at the top of almost every list (although avoiding excessive contact is also mentioned – so in terms of prayer, maybe the downside of praying for 12 hours a day would mean the kids didn't get fed). Getting to know each other, talking about the little things as well as the big things, sharing things in common – all these are important to making relationships work and they are also important to our prayer lives.

We can be so focused on only dealing with what's right in front of us that we can forget to talk to the person who is all around us. Don't get me wrong, God is not going to leave us if we forget to keep up the communication, but if we don't bother to communicate, we are responsible for the quality of the relationship at our end.

Here's a communication problem that I know I fall into. In terms of Teaspoon prayers (the TSP formula), I tend to err on the side of the P – the "please" – i.e. the asking for stuff. Where do you think the emphasis should be? Do you reckon equal time spent on all three for balance? I was greatly challenged when I heard the story of a visit of a ministry worker to an African country with Open Doors Australia. A Christian village there had been attacked by Muslim insurgents, who had massacred all the men and raped all the women. The aim had been to break the village – remove the bread-winning males, and crush the spirit of the surviving women. In the midst of their grief and shock, the women rallied. During prayer time 95% of their prayers were praise of God and 5% was asking him for things.

How confronting is that? When they had nothing, they praised God and asked for little. We have everything, and I don't know about you, but I ask for so much and give very inadequate praise. Don't get me wrong, it's not wrong to ask for things. The Bible tells us we should bring things before God by petition (Philippians 4:6), cast our anxieties on him (1 Peter 5:7) and pray without ceasing (1 Thessalonians 5:17). But we also need to remember that prayer is about praising. Prayer is worship. Psalms gives us beautiful examples of seeking and pleading and begging – as well as magnificent edifices of praise (Psalm 68 is a cracker). Let's not forget as well that when Jesus himself teaches us how to pray, he says this:

> "Our Father in heaven,
> hallowed be your name,
> your kingdom come,
> your will be done,
> on earth as it is "in" heaven.
> Give us today our daily bread.
> And forgive us our debts,
> as we also have forgiven our debtors.
> And lead us not into temptation,
> but deliver us from the evil one." (Matthew 6:9-13)

Most of what we call the Lord's Prayer is about God (*your* name, *your* kingdom, *your* will).

Going Old School and saying the Lord's Prayer has a wonderful recalibrating quality about it. It reminds us who God is. Because prayer is also about obedience. God tells us to call on him. Jesus tells us to pray. So, on one level, we just should. Here's an interesting fact though. In Deuteronomy 27:9-26, Moses recites a series of regulations building on the Ten Commandments as they have *"now become the people of the Lord your God"* (v9). Moses commands the Levites to recite the regulations and after each regulation, *"Then all the people shall say, 'Amen!'"*. This formula is repeated after each of the 12 regulations is recited. These verses give us a deeper understanding of the usage of "Amen", rather than just tailing off a prayer. It's an acceptance of each regulation. It's a show of obedience. In the face of God's will, we say "yes, truly, let it be. We accept, and we obey."

In this sense prayer is also about trust. We trust that God will sort out the details. We accept. We obey. We trust that God is sovereign and will work everything to his purposes. We accept. We obey. In our trust, we are dependent on him.

Let's pause here for a moment. That's a much bigger call than it first appears. When we pray "your will be done" do we really mean it? If we truly mean it, we should feel a little anxiety sometimes over that bit. Because what if God's will is not what I want? Now that's small beans over the little things in life, but what if it's something that really matters to you? A job decision, a home decision, a relationship decision?

Do we trust God's will enough to accept that his will is right and good? Do we trust God enough to accept his will at all?

So, if we are putting our trust in God, prayer helps us maintain a right attitude. Prayerful dependence means trust. And trust means prayerful dependence. That's putting the power where it should be. Not on us to work it out for ourselves, but on God.

To re-cap, prayer is about connecting us to God. It's about building a relationship through communication. It's about praise and worship. It's about obedience. It's about prayerful dependence and trust. And here's a big one – it's not about you. That sounds kind of high handed, doesn't it? But I say this because none of the big ideas we've talked about so far have anything to do with us. They have everything to do with God.

How can this be? How is it everything to do with God? It's not like he needs us to tell him what's going on *"for your Father knows what you need before you ask him"* (Matthew 6:8). The connecting, the relationship building, the obedience, the laying down a foundation of trust – that's all about God. In addition, if we pray without ceasing, asking God for blessing and provision, we will know far more clearly and more immediately where these things come from. If we don't ask, we will fall into the trap of thinking we did these things ourselves.

"Not to us, Lord, not to us but to your name be the glory, because of your love and faithfulness." (Psalm 115:1)

You know what's amazing though? We actually get to be part of the details. God's plans are fixed and his purposes are true. Isaiah 14:26-27 says that *"This is the plan determined for the whole world; this is the hand stretched out over all nations. For the Lord Almighty has purposed, and who can thwart him? His hand is stretched out, and who can turn it back?"*

And yet there are plenty of instances recorded in the Bible of God allowing his people to be part of the outworking. Abraham pleads for Sodom (Genesis 18:16-33) and Hannah pleads for a child (1 Samuel 1: 10-11). Yes, God is sovereign and all powerful. Yes, all things are held together by and for and through him. But we are also part of the plan. Our prayers are part of the plan. So, while you might have faith in God, you can also have faith in your own prayers. He hears them. He may not answer them the way you expect or want, but he hears them all. They are part of his plans – just like you are.

Here's where prayers get really interesting and really amazing. Prayer helps us to see the face of God. When we communicate with God with a demeanor of obedience and trust, we are more able to discern what is right and good. In 1 Chronicles 16 we see King David ministering at the Ark of the Covenant. He appoints Asaph to minister at the Ark with praise, the first verse of which is:

> *"Give praise to the Lord, proclaim his name;*
> *make known among the nations what he has done.*
> *Sing to him, sing praise to him;*
> *tell of all his wonderful acts.*
> *Glory in his holy name;*
> *let the hearts of those who seek the Lord rejoice.*
> *Look to the Lord and his strength;*
> *seek his face always."* (1 Chronicles 16:8-11)

Asaph was to do this regularly according to the day's requirements (1 Chronicles 16:37). Apart from a wonderful song of praise to God, what is clear is that seeking the face of God happens at the temple. In fact, in Isaiah, God calls his temple his "house of prayer":

> *"These I will bring to my holy mountain*
> *and give them joy in my house of prayer.*
> *Their burnt offerings and sacrifices*
> *will be accepted on my altar;*
> *for my house will be called*
> *a house of prayer for all nations."* (Isaiah 56:7)

A house of prayer for all nations. What a thing would that be? And let's not forget, Jesus quotes these words when at the temple in Matthew 21:13. We know from Matthew 26:60-62 and John 2:19 that Jesus is the new temple. If we take our 1 Chronicles passage that seeking the face of God happens at temple, then we seek the face of God in Jesus. Jesus is our house of prayer. We no longer go to a physical temple to pray. We go to Jesus in prayer.

Why I struggle with prayer

The 70s were a great time to be alive. Yes, there was sadness. I mean The Beatles broke up, there was Watergate, serial killer Ted Bundy, and Elvis Presley died, but hey, I was young and all that stuff didn't mean a thing. For me, there was disco music, a plethora of disaster movies (*Towering Inferno* was a highlight), pinafore dresses, meatloaf (not the singer) and Curly Wurleys. It was also the era that we said the Lord's Prayer every morning at school assembly. It was a normal state school, not a Christian one, and my family certainly weren't Christian. I don't think we even knew any Christians. But every morning at assembly, say it we did. But it was the *old* version so even now I have an overwhelming brain-muscle memory that makes me want to say, "Our Father in heaven, Hallowed be *thy* name, *Thy* kingdom come, *Thy* will be done".

Weird isn't it? I didn't know what it meant, but we all repeated the words. It was just something we did. I could not have even imagined that I was speaking to God, *the* God, the creator of our entire universe. I know this now, and yet still my prayer life is problematic. I know that I have a relationship with God via Jesus, and I know that any relationship that lacks communication is a pretty poor one. And yet I struggle.

There are several reasons I struggle – again, just being lazy, forgetful and unfocussed might be true, but not helpful. As with Bible reading, it is useful to look beyond the immediate and drill down on why this seems such a constant struggle. Here's what I reckon, you may have others:

It's embarrassing. When I'm on my own, I feel weird speaking out loud. When I'm in a group I feel a bit silly. I try to find the words that will make sense, that will capture the sense of the moment, that will do justice to people's prayer points, that will sound reverential and all that jazz. But then I stumble over my words, or run out of words entirely and fumble my way through to some kind of ending. Worse, if you're praying round everyone's prayer points in a circle, I spend the whole time working out which prayer point I'm going to do. Then without fail, the person next to me will do that one which sends me into a panicky mental scramble to think of another one. Of course, after all that, I haven't heard a word anyone has said, and I certainly haven't focused on God at all.

I don't really know how to do it. Take ACTS and Teaspoons. People appear to do this kind of thing seamlessly and when I first became a Christian, I was blown away. Were there classes for this kind of thing? How do people know what to say?

At the other end of the spectrum, I've been in some Pentecostal churches where prayer is much more "free form". The prayers are naturally free flowing, organic, passionate and they always build to a crescendo. There's drama. How do they know how to do that?

It's never finished. Don't get me wrong, I'm not saying that prayer is like the laundry, but I am a product of my world and I've been conditioned to have tasks that you can update to "completed". You can't tick prayer off your to-do list and so I have a mental block about doing it – I'll still have to do it tomorrow, so I'll just do it tomorrow.

It can be formulaic. This is true of my prayers on my worst days; when I know I should pray and I try but it's a very poor offering. I feel no investment, I don't feel I'm connecting with God, my words are pale and shabby, and my heart just isn't in it. Malachi 1:8 comes painfully to mind *"When you offer blind animals for sacrifice, is that not wrong? When you sacrifice lame or diseased animals, is that not wrong? Try offering them to your governor! Would he be pleased with you? Would he accept you?' says the Lord Almighty."*

It's too formal. At one point, to try and get serious about prayer, I tried to take a lot of time to do it. I wrote prayer lists (which I kept forgetting about) and I downloaded prayer apps to set an alarm for prayer time (which then just became an exercise in hand-eye coordination as I hit the Snooze button). I did learn some really important things though:

1. When you pray for a long time (i.e. give yourself a time of 30 minutes or longer) your prayers become highly thoughtful and creative. After you've been through family, your own sins, major prayer points etc., you run into trouble, so you have to allow your prayers to meander. Things pop into your head that might never have otherwise. For instance, if I can hear a mower in the distance, I pray for that guy, or for the lady at the office I say hi to because she always looks sad, or the guy I get my coffee from every morning, for that school friend from years ago that just popped into my head… and so on and so on.
2. If you manage to keep a record of your prayers, it is amazing how many of them you can see answered. When I did this, it was shocking (but not surprising) that so many were answered, and it struck me how often I pray for things and then don't even notice and praise God for his blessing. As a boost to faith though, this was huge. It was wonderful to see how clearly God was working in even the tiniest details – that he is so *big* and yet so *present* and *interested* in the minute workings of our lives.
3. From time to time, a posture of humility really changes the tone of our prayers. Praying on our knees in a physical posture of humility, reminds us of who we are before Him.

Going formal does take time and effort. But it is worth it. I kept getting distracted (two pairs of tiny hands that always want food/hugs/tissues/UN-style peace keeping force resolutions to the latest sibling fight) and that made me despondent. I am sure you have your own stresses, pressures and distractions – although to this we'll return.

It's too conversational. In an effort to boost my prayer life after trying to make them properly serious, I swung the pendulum the other way and tried to be in conversation with God throughout the day. I prayed in the car, at the shops, while I was doing little chores or in the shower. It was great. I prayed a lot more, but I ended up talking to God like he was on the end of a phone. "How can that be a bad thing?" I hear you ask. I reached the point where instead of "Amen", I said, "Okay, love you, bye." Now that could be good in that I was so used to talking to God that it became my new "normal". But in the absence of anything else, these prayers suddenly felt flippant, too shallow, lacking in... well, *awe*.

"The Lord your God is God of gods and Lord of lords, the great God, mighty and awesome." Deuteronomy 10:17

"Clap your hands, all you nations; shout to God with cries of joy. For the Lord Most High is awesome, the great King over all the earth. He subdued nations under us." Psalm 47:1-3

"The heavens declare the glory of God; the skies proclaim the work of his hands." Psalm 19:1

"OK, love you, bye." Ruth Baker

Doesn't really cut it, does it?

So where does this leave us? What are we supposed to do if our prayer life is a bit... meh?

One thing we all know is that prayer is important. The Bible tells us over and over that we should do it lots. Martin Luther said, "To be a Christian without prayer is no more possible than to be alive without breathing." – it's *that* important. Stop there and think about that for a moment. Do you pray as though it were as important to you as breathing the oxygen that keeps you alive? I don't. Maybe it's because we've forgotten what prayer is for.

I don't know if I should be praying to God or Jesus or both. Truth be told I used to get a bit confused as to whom I was praying. If we want to see the face of God, we look to Jesus, right? But then we pray to God, but in Jesus' name... wait, what? Who do I focus on? I got worried that I focussed too much on Jesus at the expense of God, but then in prayers it was all about God and Jesus was just a facilitator.

The easy answer is that we pray to God. We pray in Jesus' name as our mediator and High Priest in heaven who will always intercede for us. It's a tricky concept to wrap our brains around though because the Trinity is so difficult for us to comprehend. I try to lay that on one side for the sake of my prayers. I also try to get visual. I know that's not everyone's way of thinking, but I find imagined visual cues really help me to focus. If I close my eyes and try and imagine I am approaching the temple of Christ, I can get "into the mood". That means, the peace and quiet, the tranquillity. For others it might be that feeling of being in an empty cathedral or looking over an awe-inspiring landscape. I find my breathing starts to slow and all the chaos and mess of the day starts to get filtered out. I can imagine I am walking through the outer courtyards and allowing Jesus to lead me to God's feet where I can bow my head, praise his glorious deeds, and lay my little prayers before him. I can almost imagine Jesus kneeling with me or holding my hand and I can truly pray in his name because I can feel him with me and presenting my prayers up to our Father.

For others who are not visually oriented, it might be a more thought-driven process. Either way, it is allowing Jesus to lead you to God's feet. It is allowing that focus to take precedence in your thoughts over the noise of the day. It is calming, meditative and puts the focus on God.

I don't have faith that my prayers are working. I have talked to some people who have a hit and miss prayer life because they feel like there's no point. When you drill down on that thinking, it's not a lack of faith in God that is at issue, it's a lack of faith in themselves. How can *my* prayers help people?

This is an incredibly hard loop to get out of because it is linked to our negative self-talk that says we are failures or not worthy. It's very easy for me to say "But the prayers aren't about you, they're about God" but when it's linked so intimately to your inner voice telling you that you're a massive let down, it can be hard to keep praying.

Is this you? Do you pray (because you know you are supposed to) but deep-down feel like a fraud? This is entirely understandable. And there's not an easy fix. Can I encourage you to seek the wise counsel of Christian friends? Because that issue is less about prayer and more about your view of yourself and your self-talk. That's where Christian brothers and sisters can be an amazing sounding board and encouragement. Voice your fears to them and they can help lift you and your prayers to God. It will take time to shift your thinking. Always remember though, you haven't shifted your faith in God to faith in your own prayers, or rather our puny human ability to do anything. God is bigger. God *can* do anything.

A House of Prayer for All Nations

I think it's pretty clear by now that I'm English. Just to get it out of the way, that means I like tea in all weather and at all times of day. And it is true that English people are generally kind of grumpy and we do get pre-occupied talking about the weather. One of the things it also means is that for me, when you say "church" I picture a beautiful thousand-year-old building surrounded by crumbling gravestones. Inside there are flagstones and wooden pews and stained-glass windows. Churches feel serious and solemn. They have gravitas. They seem… well… *godly*. I have real trouble here in Australia, trying to feel the same kind of hushed awe and solemnity in a building that feels like an old scout hall. Now I know now that buildings are just buildings and God isn't any less present in a 1960's brick building than he is in a thousand-year-old edifice. But it is interesting how our surroundings can influence our feelings and thoughts when we are engaging with God.

For the Israelites in the Old Testament, if they wanted to meet God, they went to the tabernacle, or, after Solomon blew a stack of money on some building materials, at the temple in Jerusalem. Once you got past the crowds and the guys hawking animals for sacrifices, there must have been an aura of grandeur. The high walls, the towers and gates, the white stone – just the sheer scale of the thing must have been awe inspiring. And *this* is where the presence of God was. He was *actually* there. Not that the Israelites often acted like it, but he was actually *there*. In 2 Chronicles 7:1 the glory (presence) of the Lord fills the temple. Yes, he's there alright.

In those days, if you wanted to talk to God, you went to the tabernacle, and later to the temple. It was clear. That's where he was so that's where you went. Outside of that, there was nowhere to go. That was it. That's where you went. Great. Except we haven't got a temple or a tabernacle. We haven't even got a thousand-year-old impressive church type building. So how are we supposed to meet God, and sense the splendor of his glory that a temple might help to engender?

In John 1:14 we are told that the word became flesh and he dwelt among us. The word John uses for "dwelt" in the Greek he was writing in was *skénoó*. It has a deeper meaning than just "lived" or "was present" which we might think in looking at the word "dwelt". The richer Greek depths of the word relate to tent, and specifically tabernacle. And John was no fool. He knew what people would think when he used this word. He was clearly saying that Jesus "tabernacled" with us. He was the holy of holies. He was the place God dwelt among his people.

Then in John 2:18-22:

> *The Jews then responded to him, "What sign can you show us to prove your authority to do all this?" Jesus answered them, "Destroy this temple, and I will raise it again in three days." They replied, "It has taken forty-six years to*

build this temple, and you are going to raise it in three days?" But the temple he had spoken of was his body. After he was raised from the dead, his disciples recalled what he had said. Then they believed the scripture and the words that Jesus had spoken.

Jesus is the tabernacle and the temple. He fulfils both in his own body.

If we want to talk to God, this is where we go.

Create your own prayer life

What kind of person are you? Are you imaginative and creative? Task focused and organised? Whatever type of person you are, it's good to explore ways to get in touch with God as a way to focus your prayers on him. Experiment, mix and match. Some conversational prayers and some more formal prayers. Some chit chat, the occasional Lord's prayer and then from time to time, throw in prayers on your knees. Do it at the same time as your Bible reading and meditation. Do it at different times. Do it in bed, in the car, in nature, at work, in the shower, while you're out walking, while you're doing the dishes, or carve out a "nook" for yourself at home that is your special place to go. Whatever it is, it's your call. But do it. And like with Bible reading, don't give up trying. Even pray about trying. There is no limit on what we can talk to God about or ask for.

Mini-Challenge
Try praying the Lord's prayer in full every day for two weeks and afterwards dwell on one line of it each day. It could really re-ignite some important thinking on big concepts like forgiveness, trust, praise, sovereignty, obedience and acceptance.

Chapter 5
Getting My Priorities Right

What I think I should be doing:
I will prioritize church above all else

What generally happens:
Urgh! There's too much to prioritize!

The Proposition

The Proposition is that we will prioritize church above all other things in our lives. Is that a reasonable and realistic premise? In many ways, it can feel like an impossibility. We have so many things to balance, let alone prioritize. We are stretched so thin across so many competing needs. It feels like we are constantly trying to keep the plates spinning on sticks without letting any of them crash to the ground.

Turns out that the plates on sticks thing has been around about 2,000 years and was part of a Chinese proto-circus style repertoire. In the West, people were doing it from the early Middle Ages. When I was a kid, it was usually a guy in satin pants and a crushed velvet jacket dancing around to cheesy disco music while someone in the

Are we there Yet?

audience coughed uncomfortably and a ball of tumbleweed blew across the stage...

Let's face it, it's no longer a spectacular trick. Its lasting legacy is to describe how we in the modern world often feel. We have so much going on, and it feels like we have to dash around constantly to try and keep everything up there.

Is keeping a lot of plates spinning a picture of "balancing everything perfectly"? No. Anyone who pretends otherwise either has a cook and cleaner and dietician and baby-sitter, or they're faking it on Facebook. Social pressure to conform and succeed drives our felt need to look as though we're in control of everything. To not be in control appears to be a sign of weakness. We also need to keep up with everything – so we add music lessons to the soccer and the netball, we add extra tutoring and play dates and family therapy. And as the pressure gets greater, as we become more and more pressed on every side, we just run faster to keep all the plates spinning.

With so much going on in our lives is prioritizing church a reasonable proposition? Well, that's a different question.

What we need to look at is:

1. What are our "plates"?
2. Are "church" and "faith" separated in that picture?
3. Is a separation of the two important?
4. Does the state of your faith impact your attitude to church?
5. How would it look if faith and church were combined?

What are our plates?

The great thing about questioning ourselves in an analytical way is that there is no rebuke attached to them – it just acknowledges the way things are. It could be that your "plates" look something like this:

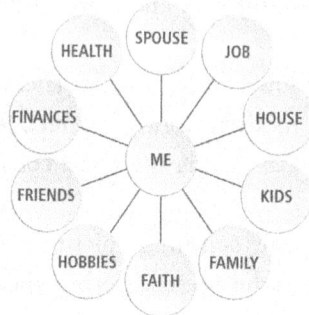

That's a lot of stuff going on. And your faith might be sandwiched between several other equally important plates.

Here's where this might present a problem for us – if everything is equally important, then nothing is important. It means the choices we make are based on what's most expedient, what's more convenient, or what can be shoe-horned in. It means our priorities are anchored in just keeping on top of everything. And no doubt – we have to manage our finances and earn money, we have to keep our kids healthy and safe, and we have to do housework. With the time left over, we might be forced then to make decisions that put our faith in direct competition with hobbies, for example. Gradually our faith gets pushed to Sunday and if we're not careful, not even then. Suddenly our plates might look more like this:

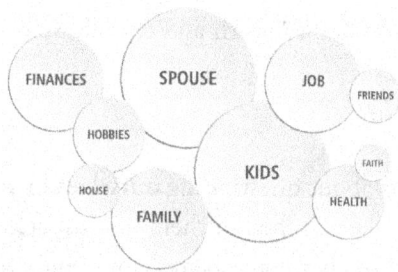

Why would this be a problem? Surely, we can all agree that while it might not be 100% reasonable, it is at least realistic? Probably, in that it is probably representative of what most of us are faced with managing in any given week. And life is complicated.

Are "church" and "faith" separated?

I often wish for simpler times. As an English person, I love watching historic English dramas on Netflix. The beautifully poetic times of 19th century England, where it always looks like a Turner painting – an orange sunny glow, hay bales, flouncy frocks, hot apple pie… Of course, we all know that isn't what England looked like, then or now. England is mostly rainy – on average nearly 150 days a year in fact. Also, in the 19th century, life expectancy was about 40-50 years, the workday could last between 10 and 18 hours (including for children) and the conditions (at work and home) were terrible. There were no health and safety policies at workplaces, no government representation for workers; there was no sanitation, little food, high infant mortality and people faced accident, death, disease and destitution most of the time. On balance, I'd say life was probably far more complicated and stressful back then. In our modern world, we just have different complications and stresses that didn't exist before.

When I say "on balance" I refer to those of us blessed with a relatively comfortable life in a safe country. This is not to ignore the high divorce rates causing enormous financial stress on single parents, the rates of those living on or below the "bread line" in every country, the high levels of domestic abuse, the shocking conditions in developing countries and the highest rates ever of slavery. But to all this we shall return in later chapters.

The complications and stresses that make me wistful for "simpler times" are things like technology, trying to fit extracurricular activities in for my kids, trying to get my kids to do their homework and trying to fit in Me Time. What I can't do is justify or discount my plate-balancing efforts as a result of life being more complicated in the modern world. I think we can see that all times have had their own complications and stresses. We just have different ones.

When things are chaotic though, we try to control things or box things in, so we can organize them better in our brains. So, this can end up happening:

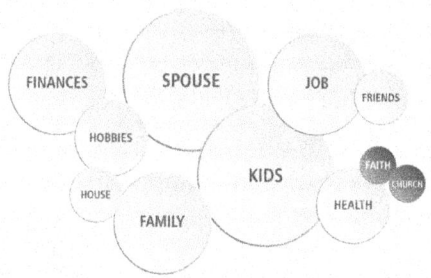

We separate "faith" and "church" – it's easier that way isn't it? Faith is something we can manage in our own way in our own time. Church has an allotted time, so it's nice and neat. It seems appropriate to separate them out anyway. We all know that God doesn't take attendance. We don't have to go to church to be saved or stay saved. It is by faith we are saved and faith alone.

But what is faith? And what is church? Why the emphasis on church rather than faith? Are they inter-dependent? This is important when we're talking about the plates on sticks thing, because too many plates means lots of crashing.

Is a separation of the two important?

In the book of Hebrews, we have the best description of "faith" – *"Now faith is confidence in what we hope for and assurance about what we do not see."* (Hebrews 11:1) Faith is knowing God is real and will deliver on his promises. It's knowing Jesus died and rose again – knowing that in our hearts and minds. Does that mean knowing it and never wavering in your faith? Does that mean never doubting anything in your faith, ever? Not necessarily, so take some pressure off. We all have doubts from time to time. You might think I would be 100% certain that the chair I am sitting on will hold my weight, but you haven't seen my capacious behind so I wouldn't be so sure.

Hardly anything substantive in our world is described in definites. Wikipedia describes a scientific theory as *"a well-substantiated explanation of some aspect of the natural world, based on a body of facts that have been repeatedly confirmed through observation and experiment. Such fact-supported theories are not 'guesses'"*. "Theory" in the scientific world is not some scientist's awesome idea that they had at 2am after drinking way too much caffeine. "Theory" is a term to describe the organization of a system of observed and substantiated facts into an explanation of natural phenomena. Because, you know… science.

We might even think of our spiritual knowledge in the same way. This is not a Science v. Faith point as the two are completely separate. Science is great at "how" things work but can only really be silent on "why". Science is not the study of cause, it can only talk about what is. So, we might equally say "God's word in the Bible is a well-substantiated explanation of the spiritual causality of the natural world, based on a body of facts that have been repeatedly confirmed through observation."[3]

---

[3] This is not an apologetics book but if you have some questions Lee Strobel's *The Case for the Resurrection* is a great start. If you are worried about your faith not being strong enough, remember, the passenger who is terrified of

Faith is knowing something enough to have it shape your world view and, most importantly, **to act on it.** If I have faith, then, it will change me somehow. If I have faith, it will influence how I see things. If I have faith, it will be visible in my behavior.

So what about church?

Church is a building used for public Christian worship. It's literally just a building. But in the New Testament, the word to describe the "church" was *ekklesia*. The word was barely used in the gospels but had general usage in Greek literature to mean "assembly" or general group of people. The word is used far more in Acts and the rest of the New Testament where clearly an assembly of people had become synonymous with a Christian gathering. So as far as the early church was concerned, the "church" was not a building – far from it, since in the early days there were no designated buildings, only small gatherings in people's homes – but a body of people.

1 Peter 2: 4-5 says, *"As you come to him, the living Stone—rejected by humans but chosen by God and precious to him—you also, like living stones, are being built into a spiritual house."* The people themselves are the building. We all – all of you reading this – are built together into a house of God.

Matthew 12:50 shows that Jesus considered the assembly as family, even saying that *"whoever does the will of my Father in Heaven is my brother and sister and mother."* As co-inheritors of God's kingdom, we are God's children. We are related. The church is family.

Maybe the most famous depiction of "church" in the New Testament is "the body" in 1 Corinthians 12. It emphasizes the unity and diversity of the gathered people of God and the different gifts they bring (i.e., the

---

flying will sit on the plane with the passenger who loves flying. Both will get where they're going because the love or fear of flying has no influence on the outcome. The disciples fear during the storm while they were on the lake had no influence on the outcome – it was Jesus who influenced the outcome.

body is made up of many parts). *"Now you are the body of Christ, and each one of you is a part of it."* (1 Cor 12:27)

What this clearly shows is that faith is *not* the same as church. But, there is a close relationship between the two, even to the point of interdependence. To take 1 Peter 2:4-5, if we are built together and we are missing from church, the building is weaker. If we are the family Jesus speaks of in Matthew 12 and we never turn up to family gatherings, the family might splinter and grow apart. If we are part of a body but we don't include ourselves in its workings, the body *might* be OK, but is more likely to get sick and wither.

Now we've already said that God doesn't take attendance, but putting "going to church" at the top of a compulsory to-do list might lead people to think that he does. If we are people of faith though, we have the kind of knowledge that means we don't just "go to church". We are part of the fabric of the church. We have a family there. We bring our gifts to the body. The Christian church has never been about a building. It has always been the people. It has always been about what people bring, just by being themselves.

Church is not what we get out of it, although in this modern climate, you could be forgiven for thinking that. We get used to thinking things like "I went to that class but I didn't get anything out of it." Viewing church as different to the "service industry" norm of the world requires some countercultural thinking. In our culture, on the one hand, we are taught not to big-note ourselves. On the other hand, our world is about individuality and the primacy of personal choice. By contrast, as Christians we can stand straight with confidence, knowing we are the children of the King. We are his treasures. His chosen ones. That's not big-noting, that's who we are. Also, as Christians, our purview is not what we get, but what we bring. Think about that. What is your church missing if you aren't there?

Faith and church together are necessary and interdependent. You can have faith without going to church, but that would mean your faith is not getting life breathed into it by the body of Christ. You can go to church without faith, but that would be only half an experience and it's not God's plan for His people to only have a partial experience of His community and kingdom.

The two together are necessary for the joyful Christian life. And I mean that in every sense of that word – fully joyous. When we allow the right wisdom to influence our thinking and decision making, it makes a lot of difference.

"*Our conscience testifies that we have conducted ourselves in the world, and especially in our relations with you, with integrity and godly sincerity. We have done so, relying not on worldly wisdom but on God's grace,*" says Paul in 2 Corinthians 1:12. Worldly wisdom tells us to stay in bed or go to the movies or go to the gym (or *not* in my case). Relying on worldly wisdom takes us to all the wrong places. God's grace takes us to church – not because God takes attendance, but because we bring something to the gathering. And we go because we have faith, we believe what the Bible tells us about how to live as Christians, and that changes our world view and influences our behavior and causes us to act.

Paul continues in verse 14 of 2 Corinthians 1, that he hopes the Corinthians "*will come to understand fully that you can boast of us just as we will boast of you in the day of the Lord Jesus*". They will boast in each other! We see here how "church" works – a mutual building up to help each other finish the race.

So in reality, "faith" and "church" are, or should be, just one of our plates on sticks, rather than two. We have seen there is a close relationship between them. But is there for you? Maybe you're reading this and thinking "that's all very well if you're an uber-Christian". Maybe you're reading this and thinking, "I have a real gap between my view of church and my faith." That's okay. Just know that you can reduce the gap, and as it reduces, your faith will be strengthened by church and your church experience will be enhanced by your faith.

In the next section, we're going to try and pin down what the gaps are, so we can look at how God tells us we can bolster each other. Then we're going to look at our plates on sticks again and how this affects how we look at life.

Does the state of your faith impact your attitude to church?

I heard "Stupid is as stupid does" in the film *Forrest Gump*. I grew up in the north of England in the 70s and 80s though, so weird sayings like this don't really phase me. In essence, this saying means that the evidence of the thing is in the action. For Forrest, when someone calls him "stupid" his mother tells him "stupid is as stupid does", meaning "if you're stupid the proof of it will be in your actions." It's up there with "the proof of the pudding is in the tasting". So, it seems fitting here to say, faith is as faith does – the proof of faith will be in your actions. But what if you're having a problem with your faith? That puts some pretty big obstacles in your way, so let's think about this a bit differently.

How would you characterize the health of your faith?

That's a pretty abstract concept so let's clarify. Felicia Huppert, director of the WellBeing Institute at the University of Cambridge and Professor of Psychology at the Institute for Positive Psychology and Education at the Australian Catholic University, has identified 10 elements of positive mental health.[4] I've add these below with a specific faith related element to help us apply it to our situation.

Element of Positive Mental Health	Definition	Faith Related Application
Positive emotions	All things considered, how happy do I feel?	How happy do I feel in my faith?

---

4   https://www.ncbi.nlm.nih.gov/pmc/articles/PMC3545194/

Engagement	Taking an interest in your work and activities	Am I interested in church services, small groups, serving at church?
Relationships	Having people in your life that you care for and who care about you	Do I have friends at church? Do I feel like I have "people"?
Meaning and purpose	Feeling that what you do in life is valuable and worthwhile	Do I feel like a valuable member of the body?
Accomplishment	Feeling that what you do gives you a sense of accomplishment and makes you feel competent	Do I feel like a good and faithful servant? Does my Bible competency give me confidence?
Emotional stability	Feeling calm and peaceful	How do I feel when I think about Jesus?
Optimism	Feeling positive about your life and your future	How do I feel when I think about church?
Resilience	Being able to bounce back in the face of adversity	How much do I worry about faith and church? Am I able to move on if things are disappointing?
Self-esteem	Feeling positive about yourself	Do I see myself as the child of the King?
Vitality	Feeling energetic	Do I love going to church? Do I love/look forward to Bible reading? Praying? Serving?

The answers to these questions will help you to pinpoint generally what the health of your faith is, and identify some more specific gaps that you might like to talk to someone about/work on with a friend/pray and meditate on to help you increase the health of your faith. For example, if you do not see yourself as the child of the King, it would be good to talk to your minister. If you don't feel like you have "people" or a community at church, maybe it's time to look at how you might make deeper relationships through Bible study, prayer couples or triplets, hospitality or serving. It's hard and it takes time, but we are already connected through Jesus which is the greatest and most secure connection anyone could have.

How would it look if faith and church were combined?

We've established that "church" and "faith" can be on one plate. We've looked too at improving the health of our faith. We still have a lot of plates though. Why do I keep banging on about this? Because it's important. It's about authentic faith –the kind of faith that is lived out by us and is clear in our actions.

Just as in the previous chapter we talked about having just one hat to take precedence over all our day-to-day hats, it's similar with plates. There is only one plate that matters. Let's drill down on this idea through a biblical lens.

> *The Lord says:*
> *"These people come near to me with their mouth*
> *and honor me with their lips,*
> *but their hearts are far from me.*
> *Their worship of me*
> *is based on merely human rules they have been taught."*
> (Isaiah 29:13)

> *"Why do you call me, 'Lord, Lord,' and do not do what I say?"* (Luke 6:46)

And, as we saw in the Introduction to this book, *"I know your deeds, that you are neither cold nor hot. I wish you were either one or the other!*

So, because you are lukewarm—neither hot nor cold—I am about to spit you out of my mouth." (Revelation 3:15-16)

Reading these makes me feel a bit queasy, because I know how rubbish I am sometimes. But that doesn't mean there's no hope for me. On the contrary, it means that I have THE hope! It means that I am aware enough to know that my faith feels bigger and smaller at different times, my ability to be an integral member of the church community ebbs and flows. Some days I'm awesome at reading my Bible and praying and other days I am terrible at it. I always forget to lay things before God when I have a big problem or decision to make, and more often than not will dive in and try and solve it myself. There are so many different ways my other plates take priority and push the main plate down the chain.

But this also means I have to keep trying. We can't be perfect all the time. We can't be perfect at any time, that's the whole point of God having to send Jesus. So, knowing that perfection is not a factor, trying becomes the best attainable standard. Which really takes the pressure off, right?

Matthew 6:25-34 is brilliant. I mean, it's all good, but this bit is a real gem. It's the bit where Jesus is talking about worry.

> *"Therefore I tell you, do not worry about your life, what you will eat or drink; or about your body, what you will wear. Is not life more than food, and the body more than clothes? Look at the birds of the air; they do not sow or reap or store away in barns, and yet your heavenly Father feeds them. Are you not much more valuable than they? Can any one of you by worrying add a single hour to your life?*
>
> *"And why do you worry about clothes? See how the flowers of the field grow. They do not labor or spin. Yet I tell you that not even Solomon in all his splendor was dressed like*

> one of these. If that is how God clothes the grass of the field, which is here today and tomorrow is thrown into the fire, will he not much more clothe you—you of little faith? So do not worry, saying, 'What shall we eat?' or 'What shall we drink?' or 'What shall we wear?' For the pagans run after all these things, and your heavenly Father knows that you need them. But seek first his kingdom and his righteousness, and all these things will be given to you as well. Therefore do not worry about tomorrow, for tomorrow will worry about itself. Each day has enough trouble of its own."

We worry about all the plates we have to keep spinning – all the money we have to earn, the house we have to keep, the job we have to perform, the problems we have to solve, the issues we have to work out, the family we have to serve... none of these things is wrong in and of itself. But if we truly believed that God was sovereign, would we worry? We worry about things we can't control. We worry about things that God *is* in control of. So if we worry, it means we are not trusting God – not deliberately, not with forethought or malice, it's just our natural way of operating. It is desperately difficult to let things go to God once, let alone to keep doing it. We have very short memories and I don't know about you, but every time I get into a fix, by the time I give it all up to God (and then feel a million times better having done it), I kick myself that I didn't think to do it before.

Seek his kingdom first, it says in verse 33. Have one plate and one stick, he may as well have said. (Okay. Jesus said it better.)

How do you only have one plate? It's about bringing things into line. It's about seeking the kingdom first. So instead of having a whole line of plates you need to keep spinning, there is one plate on which everything else sits. The plate itself is our faith/church life and everything else sits on top - our faith underpins everything else. So instead of this:

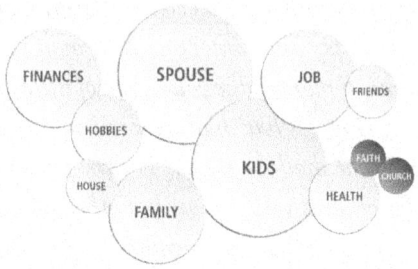

We aim to have something like this:

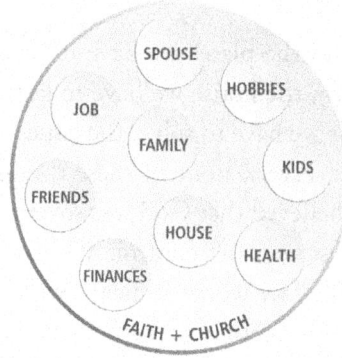

Bringing these into line might take some thought and effort. There might be difficult choices that need to be made. There might be things that you want to start doing because you'd never thought to do them before. There might be things you need to stop doing. Rethinking your plates so that they now sit on top of this most significant of plates requires some critical assessment though. For each of our plates, we need to assess "What would this plate look like if I was Christian first, and this second?"

For example, maybe at work, you never talk about being a Christian, maybe you even "check it at the door". What might it look like if you were Christian first?

What would my house look like if I was Christian first? Should it be used more for hospitality?

This process is about choices we make. And choices can be easy, or they can be hard. Making these choices will lead to a clarity about what's important, it will align our lives with Scripture, it will help us to build up our authentic faith – and hopefully that of others too. Making these choices will help us to stay focused on what is of the most importance. When your whole life is channeled through Christ, it's hard not to stay focused. When we're constantly thinking about how to do life, we constantly course correct as we need to.

I get really inspired by people who have made much harder choices than I ever have – and it helps to put my puny little choices into perspective. Eric Liddell was a Scottish Olympian (for those of you over 40 he was the *Chariots of Fire* guy). In the 1924 Paris Olympics, he declined to run in the 100m heats which were held on a Sunday. It was his best event but he chose not to run it. He chose devotion to Jesus and his active faith over a gold medal. The following year, instead of continuing to compete, he gave it all up to become a missionary in China.

Lillias Trotter was an aspiring artist in the late 19th century. A leading art critic of her day, John Ruskin, told her that if she dedicated herself to her art, she could be the greatest living painter. Lillias decided she could not give her life to art and at the same time, seek first the kingdom of God. She gave up art and focused on Christian works of compassion in London and then journeyed to north Africa as a missionary.

My choices are far more subdued. My choices are about whether to see less of some friends because I get drawn into gossip. They are about whether I share what happened at church with the non-Christian people in my life. They are about whether to open my home more to host small groups or to help new church members to forge relationships. Hardly giving everything up for the kingdom.

Ultimately though, my choices need to lead me to aligning my life with my faith first. What would your life look like if you only had one plate to worry about? How would you feel if you could confidently stop watching TED Talks on time management and work-life balance and focus instead on just your one plate?

"The path of the righteous is like the morning sun, shining ever brighter till the full light of day." (Proverbs 4:18)

Chapter 6 ─────────────────────
You Are What You Eat

> ***What I think I should be doing:***
> *I will read Christian books that are edifying and nourishing*
>
> ***What generally happens:***
> *I'll just do this other thing over here…*

The Proposition

The proposition is that we, as Christians, will only read, listen to and talk about things that are good for us – that is, edifying and nourishing for our souls. This assumes we are capable of a level of single-mindedness and purity that (let's face it) is super-human. But we also understand the concept of "junk in, junk out". We understand this concept in terms of our bodily health. "If I eat healthily" we think, "it will be better for me." And we'd be right.

The same should work for our spiritual health. "If I read/watch/listen to this thing and not that thing" we think, "then I will be spiritually stronger." And, again, we'd be right. It's a relatively straightforward concept – healthy input, healthy output. Or: Junk in, junk out. If I eat nothing but chocolate bars and chips, I will end up with a horribly unhealthy heart. If I watch nothing but R-rated movies, my heart will be affected by this too. And that will display itself though my language, behavior and attitudes. It may even start to skew my perspective towards my faith and obedience to God.

This is not a new concept. Human attention is always prone to wander:

"You are the salt of the earth. But if the salt loses its saltiness, how can it be made salty again? It is no longer good for anything, except to be thrown out and trampled underfoot." (Matthew 5:13)

What is this "saltiness"? It can mean its flavor and its purpose – the purpose of salt is to enhance the flavor of food. In addition, in the Old Testament, the Israelite's relationship with God is described as "A covenant of salt". This has some cultural meaning in the Middle East. There is an ancient Arabic expression: "There is salt between us." It comes from the fact that covenants were confirmed over table fellowship, and salt was always present at these meals. In addition, there is the symbolic component; salt represents the preservation of the covenant.[5]

If the salt relates to the Old Testament understanding of the word and is symbolic of our covenant with God, we are being told that we are the sign of the covenant on earth. We are the salt.

Here is the danger for us though. There are only two ways that salt can lose its saltiness. It becomes corrupted with another substance, or it becomes diluted with water. And what good is salt if it loses its saltiness by corruption or dilution? It is useless. It doesn't do what it was designed to do. In the same way, our Christian lives lose their potency if we become corrupted or diluted. We become, effectively, useless. We are not doing what we are designed to do.

In summary, this essentially means, "You are the sign of God's

---

[5] I flesh out these ideas in an article for GoThereFor.com called "A fun fact in Leviticus that helps us lead full lives". https://gotherefor.com/offer.php?intid=29733

covenant on earth. But if you cease to be a living symbol of God's glory and promise, you are not doing what you are designed to do."

And we know all too well that our Christian lives can become corrupted or diluted with other materials. This is stuff that looks like salt but is actually flour or chalk dust or sugar. These are the things we include in our lives that may not be bad in and of themselves, but which – individually or aggregated – make our salt a lot less salty.

Our Christian lives can also be made less salty by damp that seeps in and drains salt of its taste and purity. This might occur via things in our lives that we don't even notice – the effect of TV, social media, friends and acquaintances, our work environment – subtle environmental elements that slowly drip, drip, drip into our lives. Before you know it, your thinking has changed, your decisions are less focused, your choices are less discerning. You put up with more of what you used to distance yourself from: poor language; extra drinks at the pub; gossip or malicious slander; music, TV and films with unhealthy values. That's what becoming less salty looks like. You start to become less distinguishable from the world.

But why is it so difficult?

If "healthy input, healthy output" rather than "junk in, junk out" is the key to spiritual health, why do we need a whole chapter on this? It seems so simple. Well, I don't think it's as simple as it seems. I think we put an awful lot of pressure on ourselves to just do things better. "I must read more edifying things" we think, "and stop listening to that pop star and watching those TV shows." Yet here we are again on a Friday night, watching the latest TV show that celebrates people being horrid to each other, and then that film that's full of swearing and violence. Except now I feel ashamed. Now I feel like a failure.

So, is the Proposition reasonable, given that it seems so difficult to achieve? I would like to think so, even though I know it will lie somewhere between the ideal and the reality.

It is a reasonable thing to strive for. Jesus explained this in no uncertain terms to the religious leaders of the day. The leaders had been focusing on legalistic attitudes to food laws and Jesus set them straight on where true purity lies, saying *"Don't you see that whatever enters the mouth goes into the stomach and then out of the body? But the things that come out of a person's mouth come from the heart, and these defile them. For out of the heart come evil thoughts—murder, adultery, sexual immorality, theft, false testimony, slander. These are what defile a person; but eating with unwashed hands does not defile them."* (Matthew 15:17-20,)

It is this approach to inner purity that finds its outworking in James 4:7-8: *"Submit yourselves, then, to God. Resist the devil, and he will flee from you. Come near to God and he will come near to you. Wash your hands, you sinners, and purify your hearts, you double-minded."*

So yes, this is a reasonable thing to strive for. If we are to have a strong and glorifying relationship with God, we need to be single-minded in our approach to personal purity. Our words, behavior, attitudes, choices and actions are the fruit of our hearts. What we treasure – good or bad – will determine what fruit we will bear. Healthy input, healthy output. Junk in, junk out.

But, if it's that simple, why is it so difficult? Is it because we have lost our attention spans? Are we victims of our own modern era? We have so many things clamoring for our attention, it seems impossible to filter out the rubbish and focus on what is edifying.

Have we moved beyond simple edifying material because we are surrounded by gossip and excitement and drama? By comparison, "edifying" can become the same in our minds as "boring". With limited time in our busy world, we tend to choose exciting over boring every time.

Is it too hard? Sometimes "edifying" can also mean "a chore". At the end (or really, at any time) of the day, my brain is full and any inputs other than kids and my job tend to be chosen on the basis of how easy it is to digest. Should I read something edifying that might take a bit more effort to read? Or should I flick through that magazine over there?

Sometimes I try and cut myself a bit too much slack and let myself off the hook. "I'm a product of my culture," I think, "life is just faster and busier than ever before. If I was living in a convent then, yeah, sure. I could devote hours to quiet worship of God that is focused and single-minded. But I live in the real world. So maybe I'll just flick through the magazine before I have to do the next thing…"

The trouble with this thinking is the fact that Jesus – and the writers of the rest of the Bible – spent a good deal of time talking about this. Which means that the audience 2,000 years ago, who were also a product of their culture, struggled with this as well. I don't mean they faced the same media as we do, or the same influx of information. I mean they struggled to make the right choices too. They struggled to choose what was spiritually nourishing over what was unhealthy.

This is not a modern-era problem, this is a human problem.

That said, we can't ignore how our culture is shaping us – sometimes without us even knowing it. We need to be able to dissect our environment in order to understand where our triggers lie. If we can start doing this, maybe we can start recognizing when we are making good choices, and when we are making poor ones, and, prayerfully, start making more of the good ones.

So how do we get to grips with this so we can start making more informed choices?

There are two key ways that we get our "food". First, we get our nourishment from the crumbs that are all around us. It's our culture. That means it's in the air we breathe – these are the things we haven't directly chosen, but we take in without even realizing it. Secondly, we get our "food" from the things we specifically choose.

In this chapter, we are going to aim to do two things:

1. Understand our culture and environment a bit more – almost like trying to explain a magic trick. Once the trick is explained, it is de-mystified. If something is de-mystified, we know what it is and how we can approach it, think about it and manage it.
2. Look at being a product of God, rather than culture, and how we are actually supposed to live this out.

It is worth saying here that the process of de-mystifying is so we can better manage our place in the world. This is not separate to our relationship with Jesus or our salvation (which we already have). Nor does it negate the work that the Holy Spirit is doing in us. This process of self-reflection is designed to help us to know what to pray for and where we can specifically ask the Spirit for guidance and help and strength.

Our culture will always work against us. We are Christian after all. And, seeing that we have salvation and are striving to live a life worthy of our calling, and grow in Christ-likeness with the help of the Spirit, understanding the barriers and issues in front of us can help us to do that more seamlessly.

What is the culture we are a product of?

Let's deal with our culture first, because it's a big shapeless concept that's quite heard to pin down. It is a critical question though – If we are a product of our culture which molds how we think and influences the choices we make, what is culture?

Culture is defined by the beliefs and behaviors of a group of people who are linked by common characteristics and a general idea of what the purpose of that society is. So, we could say that a church has a culture, and the culture of a church could be different to the culture of a workplace. Those are specific micro-cultures though. What I am talking about here is the bigger picture. What's in the air that we breathe? What's the soup we swim in? And other great metaphors like that.

This is where it can be tricky because cultures differ across the world. Culture in Sydney will be different to Kuala Lumpur, just as London and New York culture will differ to that of Cape Town. So, let's make the distinction between "society" and "culture" to help us explain it better.

Culture and Society

Our "society" is the building blocks. It's the scaffolding. For example, your town might be the scaffolding – it's just a town, like any other – with streets and shops and schools and parks and so on.

Our "culture" is what defines the town as different to other towns. It's what fills in the empty spaces. This is important because it helps us start to pick apart what "product of our culture means", which helps us then to start seeing what in our atmosphere we are letting seep into our spiritual lives.

Here are some of the basic but commonly recognized defining features of a society with some examples that fit for our Western world but could easily be replaced with local examples. As you read this list, have a think about what the building blocks of your personal society are:

Society "scaffolding"	Culture examples
Customs	Easter, Christmas, public holidays (particularly those including get-togethers and BBQs), celebrating birthdays, engagement parties and weddings (including wedding lists, gift giving, bucks and hens nights), christenings (even when not Christian). At most of these there are certain food and drink associations (Easter eggs, turkey, cake) and community attachments (when family gathers or when best friends come together) that become anchor points in the rhythms or our year.
Norms	Norms to us might be a basic expectation of health care and education as well as human and personal rights.
Rules	This can include laws and regulations as well as expectations of fairness and justice. There are social rules, or rules about being in the workplace for example.

So, if society is the scaffolding, culture is the things that enhance the basic structure.

Culture and Values

Culture is also defined by shared values. What we value as a group of people can be one of those elements that fills in the gaps in our society scaffolding.

It can be hard to pinpoint what these values are because we (as humans) are so diverse. So, an interesting way to look at this is through things that we have in common. For example, where we spend our money. This too was a subject of the teaching of Jesus. Here is one of his most profound teachings about money:

"Do not store up for yourselves treasures on earth, where moths and vermin destroy, and where thieves break in and steal. But store up for yourselves treasures in heaven, where moths and vermin do not destroy, and where thieves do not break in and steal. For where your treasure is, there your heart will be also." (Matthew 6:19-21)

Do not focus on worldly wealth, but on eternity, because what we gather and cling to reveals where our heart really is. A preoccupation with money is not a modern concern! Money had (and still has) value in and of itself, and value for what it means and can do in our lives. And what does it do in our modern lives? What is it that *we* value?

In Australia, the Bureau of Statistics showed that in 2015-2016, after housing, transport and food, we spend the most on recreation.[6] We spend more on recreation alone than we do on fuel and utilities and health. What is interesting is that this is the case for high, middle and low-income earners. I know how that sounds. I took a bit of offense myself. I run a tight budget and I was a bit put out at the idea that I was over the top with my spending on "recreation". Don't be put out – this is the *general* trend. This is looking at what we do on average as a collection of people in the same society. This is balanced with Australians giving less than 1% to charity. Again, some people give far more than that, but this is a general trend across our society.[7] So as a society, we use our money to survive, and with what is left, we tend to spend it on things for our personal enjoyment.

---

[6] http://www.abs.gov.au/ausstats/abs@.nsf/Latestproducts/6530.0Main%20Features42015-16?opendocument&tabname=Summary&prodno-6530.0&issue=2015-16&num=&view=

[7] https://www.smh.com.au/business/the-economy/australias-charitable-giving-jumps-65-per-cent-national-australia-bank-20160426-gof5vs.html

This can also be seen in how advertisers reflect back to us what we value. Or, more to the point, what the advertisers *want us* to think we value. In 2017 in Australia alone, nearly $14.5 billion was spent on advertising.[8] The top advertisers were Wesfarmers (which includes Coles), Woolworths, Reckitt Benckiser (which includes Dettol, Harpic, Calgon and other stuff you'd find under the kitchen sink), McDonalds, Toyota, Harvey Norman and Telstra. Retail (excluding food) and motor vehicles top the market share though.[9] So, basically, *stuff*.

This stuff becomes the air we breathe, and we get sucked into the idea that we need it to survive. "If I have that stuff", we think, "life will somehow be *better*."

So – our society is merely the building blocks. Our culture is the cement that glues it together. Part of that culture is expressed in what we value and one of the things we value is money, and more particularly what that money represents and what we think it will get us. We – and the advertisers – think it will buy us happiness. So we might value "happiness" and happiness as a pursuit is an important part of our culture. This pursuit makes up a large part of the air we breathe, and the types of culture we take into our brains and that shapes our hearts.

Happiness is elusive. Why is that? Is it because we are built to be discontent with our lot? Is it because we have been trained to always want more? Or is there something else going on? Well, it's a bit of everything.

As humans, we are prone to wander. We seem to have a short memory when it comes to blessing. God was actually with the Israelites in the desert and yet they still whined and complained. We also have an in-built tendency to covet. Isn't it interesting that coveting made it to the 10 big ones that Moses brought down from Mount Sinai? Coveting

---

[8] https://www.statista.com/statistics/237934/australian-advertising-expenditure/

[9] http://www.adnews.com.au/news/where-s-the-money-going-exclusive-ad-spend-trends-report

doesn't sound that bad compared to murder. But coveting is a darkness in the heart that casts shade over everything we do. We become jealous and petty when we live by comparison with others. You could have a perfectly good life but as soon as you compare yourself to the next guy, something won't stack up. Then suddenly your motivation is about doing things to get things – and getting things to be happy. Filling a hole in your life, with stuff – because you don't have it and because someone else does.

This is the very anxiety that ad-people have exploited forever. Because we are human and sinful, we are particularly receptive to advertising. And then our natural inclinations become honed and shaped and trained to want more. We have willingly placed ourselves into an economy of discontent. The more we feel discontent, the more we want, the more we'll buy. And yet we are still not happy, we are still discontent… and then the cycle just begins again. Because what we have is never enough.

Proverbs 30:15-16 says that:

> *"The leech has two daughters.*
> *'Give! Give!' they cry.*
> *"There are three things that are never satisfied,*
> *four that never say, 'Enough!':*
> *the grave, the barren womb,*
> *land, which is never satisfied with water,*
> *and fire, which never says, 'Enough!'*

The four things we can picture and understand clearly enough. People will (until Jesus returns) always die. So the grave will never be full. We can all understand and sympathise with a woman's insatiable and anguished yearning for a child. We all know what happens when you don't water the land. I have three plants at my front door and every time I pass their withered and wilted skeletons I think "But surely I only just watered you yesterday!" And yet today, again, they need water. And fire will consume as long as there is flammable material to burn.

The "headline act" though is the leech's two daughters. The leech is a blood-sucker and so is shown here as the very epitome of insatiable greed. The daughters of the bloodsucker keep crying for more. That's us I'm afraid. God knew it – he knows us so well! That's why this passage is here in Proverbs. He is teaching us wisdom in an area that is so natural to us!

Discontent is natural to us – but it's also because we assume that happiness is a constant state. This is what Hollywood has taught us. There's a happy ending, the scene fades to credits and the happiness is perfectly preserved forever as a constant state of emotional bliss. But we know that life is not really like that. There are months where we don't quite meet all our financial needs. There are arguments with the kids over getting out of the door on time. The dinner burns. Work is horrible. Someone is mean. Happiness is not a constant state. And yet that is what we keep striving for, thinking it is possible, and feeling short changed when we don't have it.

In many ways now, happiness has become a by-product of acquisition of things or the completion of tasks, goals and projects (whether it be a promotion at work or a walk in the country) that we attach emotional value to. The pursuit of happiness triggers our dopamine (which we talked about in Chapter 1 as our reward center of the brain). A chemical reward for anticipating getting what we want actually keeps our sense of discontent alive. We cannot have anticipation of reward without wanting something. And we don't want something unless we are discontent – unless we are lacking something.

Our sense of achievement, once attained, floods us with adrenalin or euphoria which we equate with happiness. But it's just a chemical in the body. And it's not a constant. It floods the body, it does its job (increases the heart rate, activates neurotransmitters and all that jazz) and then it recedes. The discontent-anticipation-acquisition reward cycle just keeps going.

Here's some more bad news. Lots of clever people including everyone from psychologists to economists, have discovered that we humans adapt to our circumstances. We get our new thing or achieve our next goal, but then we adapt and habituate to our new circumstances and our happiness level reverts to where it was before. For example, I work towards my dream house. I get it. I am happy. Then in time I adapt and habituate. Gradually my "happiness level" becomes what it was before. "Clearly," wrote economist Richard Layard, "the secret of happiness is to seek those good things that you can never fully adapt to."[10]

As Christians, these are the choices we face every day. When we allow ourselves to be part of the economy of discontent, we are choosing the soup that we swim in. We are choosing to swim in the same soup as the rest of the world. The "rest of the world" is the culture and society of which we are a product.

Here's what Jesus said:

"The eye is the lamp of the body. If your eyes are healthy, your whole body will be full of light. But if your eyes are unhealthy, your whole body will be full of darkness. If then the light within you is darkness, how great is that darkness!"

"No one can serve two masters. Either you will hate the one and love the other, or you will be devoted to the one and despise the other. You cannot serve both God and money." (Matthew 6:22-24)

Our culture is built on keeping our eyes dark. The search for happiness is a preoccupation in our culture. It becomes a purpose in and of itself. Whole societal building blocks have been shaped by this concept. Our customs have become commercially driven. Our basic expectations have started including non-essential items – free parking

---

[10] Richard Layard, *Happiness. Lessons from a New Science*, Penguin Books, 2005.

and WiFi have become as important as health care and education. The cultural dressing in between the building blocks is focused on the search for happiness. Making more money, how we spend it, how we show it off – and what choices we make to become (what we think is) *happy*. This then has a ripple effect through *all* the choices we make and *why*.

Your life, starring You

So far, we've focused on society and culture. Now we need to look at ourselves – or rather, ourselves as individuals who are a product of what we've discussed so far.

What is interesting is that our culture and society make us individual, isolated, self-seeking, survival of the fittest type people. And yet, there is still something deeply sown in all of us that sits uneasily with what culture would have us be. Here's a clue as to some of our deepest yearnings:

The three top-selling books of all time are *Don Quixote* (500 million), *A Tale of Two Cities* (200 million) and *The Lord of The Rings* (150 million). They are stories of redemption, of the triumph of good over evil, of light overcoming darkness. Stories of epic quests and finding strength. Stories of being a *hero*.

This is where the heart of the issue lies. We want to be part of a community. We want to belong. We want to be part of a purpose that is bigger than ourselves and we want to be *in* the narrative. With every story, we imagine ourselves into the narrative. It's why advertising works so well – we can imagine being that person. The most enduring stories are the ones that reflect what we truly yearn for.

Don Quixote is a man who loses himself so much in chivalric stories that it takes him over and he sets out to revive chivalry and right wrongs. *A Tale of Two Cities* is set against the backdrop of the French Revolution and traces the redemption of a drunk lawyer and the triumph of love over all. *The Lord of The Rings* is an epic battle against evil, against all odds, by a band of unlikely heroes.

What is so profoundly important in all this is that this is exactly what God would have for us. He wants us to be redeemed and to right wrongs, he wants us to be part of something bigger, he wants us to be a community.

In his second letter to the Corinthians, Paul discusses the church's unity in diversity at some length. *"Now you are the body of Christ, and each one of you is a part of it."* (1 Corinthians 12:27) In movie terms, we are an "ensemble cast". That doesn't mean that we become lost in the crowd though. We still have a part to play. We all have a narrative that is personal to our life, even though it makes up part of the whole bigger story. And Christ hasn't left us un-equipped to be part of something bigger. As Paul explains to the Ephesians *"we are God's handiwork, created in Christ Jesus to do good works, which God prepared in advance for us to do."* (Ephesians 2:10) In describing the work of the community, Paul, in his first letter to the Corinthians, had shown how different people have different roles, but, in his letter to the Ephesians, he shows us that it is God himself who has written and is directing our story.

As an ensemble cast of believers, in all our diversity, we have a common purpose. We have one goal. *"For we are co-workers in God's service; you are God's field, God's building."* (1 Corinthians 3:9)

What God wants for us sits far more easily with our natural yearnings. What we yearn for does not fit with where our culture leads us. It does, however, fit with where God leads us. With one, we will feel dissatisfied and out of step. With the other, we will feel whole and purposeful. So we should live for the latter. Not the former. Live for God, not for the world.

Being a Product of God, Not of Culture

Great. But what does that look like?

Have a look at some of the thought steps in this chapter – the building blocks of your society, the cultural gap fillers, what your personal narrative is. Dissecting society and culture is a helpful exercise in identifying what "we eat" every day that we don't even realise.

Since this is the air we breathe, perhaps without even realizing it, it becomes more important than ever that we map our surroundings and are aware of the influences that pervade our whole lives. This is what shapes our thinking. This is what molds our decision-making process. This can be (if we let it) one of the reasons making the right choices about what we "eat" is so difficult.

This determines what our "light in the darkness" is.

This will establish how many masters we have.

This will regulate what we treasure and what we store up in our barns.

Critically assess your life and what you can see of the things that are influencing how you are spending your time and your money. Then pray and ask God to show you how those factors shape your decision-making. Here are some questions that might help you to critically assess the building blocks in your personal landscape:

- What drives me?
- What do I value?
- Are there things that I do in order to impress others?
- Are there things I do in order to shore up my own confidence in myself?
- When I feel unsure, what is my light in the darkness?
- What do I turn to for comfort?

Maybe there are things you should be making decisions about that you aren't. These might be things that you go along with because you don't even notice them. They might be things you only notice because you are deliberately assessing your surroundings. They might be things that you know are there, but you don't make a decision about because you don't know where to start.

Ask God for wisdom to see where you should be making decisions. And then ask him to help you make decisions that honour him. Because there are always decisions we can make. They might not be obvious or easy, but even the biggest global ideas become personal choices in our homes and in our hearts. There is always an element under our control that we can seek God's wisdom in.

So what are we supposed to do?

What are we to do with all this?

First of all, remember that we are saved by grace through faith in Christ alone. We must always remember that. It's easy for us to look at our blind spots and come up with a list of things to do. But then our focus can become so myopic that we end up replacing God's own good and eternal works and purposes for us, with our own puny works/tasks/spiritual checklist.

This is always a helpful corrective when we are looking at how to live life in a manner consistent with our faith and calling.

That said, we can focus on the "how" of our salted life. A salted life is a pure life, the life that is a sign of God's covenant in your corner of the world. This is the life that reflects God's glory back to him. This is the life that other people look at and see a picture of God at work. This is where people will see faith in action.

Where are the points in your world where you are, or should be, counter cultural? Do you need to change, avoid or cut some things out?

Do you need to have a think about your attitude to some things that you hadn't previously considered? Are there some things that you want to be more intentional about, particularly in parenting choices? In how you communicate with your partner? With how you conduct yourself at work?

Then there's the more visible culture, the things we choose to interact with. There are choice points throughout our day that lead us to a holistic approach to being a product of God:

- What radio station do I listen to?
- What TV shows do I watch?
- What books do I read?
- How much TV do I watch?
- What food do I eat?
- How much time do I spend on social media?

The two key questions are "what?" and "how much?" "What?" is not necessarily as easy as it looks. There are TV programs for instance, that are not bad, but bad enough to make us numb to their effects on us. Also, sometimes we don't really realise what's around us. While in the car, I hummed along (loudly and *beautifully*) to a Katy Perry song. It was a song I'd hummed along to for ages. But this time, I actually listened to the words. Oh. *Oh...* I changed stations.

In addition, even good things can become bad things if we have too much of them. Watching TV can be great down time. Watching it for 5 hours has probably stopped me doing something with the kids, from reading a book, from going for a walk, from meeting friends, from working on a hobby, from cooking a healthy dinner.

These are the choices we make. What am I "eating"? What is influencing me? Is my saltiness being corrupted? Is my saltiness being diluted? What choices can I make to improve it? Am I aware of it?

Awareness is the first step. I can't be the only one who's hummed along to a song that I wouldn't want my kids listening to, without even realising it.

I talked previously about mapping your culture and society and then critically assessing it. What are the things you notice? What are the visible markers of your world? Are they good for you? How do they affect you? How do they subtly influence you?

Next, do a bit of a stock-take of your daily choice points – when you get in the car, when you get to work, when you drop off the kids at school, all those points where you *choose* what to see or read or hear or be a part of. Are there some different choices to be made?

Be intentional. Once you've looked at the "micro" picture of your daily choices, then sit back and dwell and pray. Don't think necessarily about the small choices you need to make but what kind of person you want to be. If you want to be a salted person, that means being a visible sign of God's covenant. What would that look like for you? Some of it will already be happening as the Holy Spirit sanctifies and shapes and changes you in your Christian journey. But maybe there are some areas you need to consider more and ask God for the Holy Spirit's help to change them.

Be aware though, that this isn't easy. There are many things in our culture that we are addicted or habituated to. Making some choices will be hard. But they don't have to be drastic and complete. We are a fellowship. Seek help. Pray to God. Seek him in his word. We all know that if we eat junk food, we'll be sick and our body won't work well.

We also know that if we eat healthy food, our bodies will work well and our hearts will pump strongly.

If we can understand our surroundings and start to make better choices about what we let into our minds and hearts, we will grow in strength and vitality, pointing people to God, and becoming more resilient and joyful on our Christian journey.

Remember though – we have been de-mystifying our culture. We have not been de-mystifying God. God rules over all and is in control of all. This is where we get to express our obedience though: in the choices we make. As you reflect on this chapter, remember to keep praising God, and asking him for the help of the Spirit where you can see you have difficult areas.

Chapter 7
It Takes a Village

> ***What I think I should be doing:***
> *I will be part of a community of believers, who share our whole lives for the sake of Christ*
>
> ***What generally happens:***
> *I'd much rather be left alone to do my own thing*

The Proposition

The Proposition is that as Christians, we will be, and are, part of a community of believers who share our whole lives for the sake of Christ. It's not that we are part of a cult, but that we are united by a special bond and that our community comes first – even above family. We get this picture from Jesus himself who makes a clear statement about how we should view the Christian community.

"*While Jesus was still talking to the crowd, his mother and brothers stood outside, wanting to speak to him. Someone told him, 'Your mother and brothers are standing outside, wanting to speak to you.' He replied to him, 'Who is my mother, and who are my brothers?' Pointing to his disciples, he said, 'Here are my mother and my brothers. For whoever does the will* of my Father in heaven is my brother and sister and mother.'" (Matthew 12:46-50)

This places a lot of pressure on church relationships. Indeed, you might wonder if you are willing to get involved considering the kinds of rights and obligations this describes. Most of us already have so many people in our lives who want or need something from us. After everyone has taken their piece of us, we just want to be left alone. And what about people who are more difficult to relate to?

So often on Facebook we'll see memes like:

> "I refuse to entertain negativity. Life is too big and time is too short to get caught up in empty drama."

> "You cannot hang out with negative people and expect to live a positive life."

> "Protect your spirit from contamination. Limit your time around negative people."

> "Cutting people off doesn't have limits. Family can get cut off too if they're causing you stress. Eliminate any negativity from your circle."

When did this become a thing? When did cutting people out of our lives if they are too difficult to be around become a thing?

How did the biblical view that all believers are to be like family become so divergent from the worldly view?

"Isolationism" is a political term. It describes a foreign policy built around leaving everyone else to deal with their own problems. It's been employed by countries in both the East and the West. For example, the United States went through a stronger period of isolationism after World War I and the Great Depression. These were incredible tragedies and pressures and so the response was understandable. The aim was to make them stronger as a people and a country, building on their own resources, and becoming more self-reliant. Unfortunately, a knock-on effect of an isolationist approach is also to become suspicious of outsiders. Looking inward creates a view that there are enemies outside. This is the same whether you're the US or Australia or Bhutan or Turkey – the effects will look slightly different, but eventually it will lead to the same ends.

As people, we tend to respond to pressure the same way. We hunker down. We keep ourselves to ourselves.

To be fair, this is how we all respond to culture. And our culture is isolationist. It's about the individual. Since the 1940s, the number of people living alone in Australia has increased sharply to a quarter of our population. This is not the highest in the world but it is by no means the lowest, and a marked increase from less than 10% living alone in the early 40s.[11] Whether living alone or not, a recent Relationships Australia survey found that around a quarter of respondents felt left out, and over a third felt they lacked companionship. A third felt isolated often and a further 43% felt isolated sometimes. That's over 80% who felt isolated by varying degrees from sometimes to always.[12] Over 80%! Tragically, in their 2011 Relationship Indicators Report, while 35% of respondents sought help from friends and family, and 22% sought professional help when needed, 23% tried to work it out themselves or simply didn't know what to do.[13]

It will also come as no surprise that 81% of teenagers in the US were using social media in 2016, which is up from 55% in 2006, and

---

[11] https://aifs.gov.au/publications/demographics-living-alone#figure1
[12] https://www.relationships.org.au/what-we-do/research/online-survey/january-2017-loneliness
[13] https://www.relationships.org.au/what-we-do/research/australian-relationships-indicators/relationships-indicator-2011/view

74% of adults are now on social media, compared to just 8% in 2006.[14] In some ways, social media can increase feelings of connection. It can increase people's contact with friends and especially family (speaking as an English person living in Australia, I can attest to this!). But there's a downside. In 2014, a UK charity, Scope, conducted a survey and found that social media made 62% of people feel inadequate, 60% feel jealous and 30% feel lonely.[15]

We don't need statistics to tell us that times have changed. Modern society has seen ever increasing social movement, so that people no longer spend their lives in the same community, living close to their families. We can all feel that we've lost something. What we've gained in amazing technology and social advancement and the breaking down of barriers, has meant a commensurate dismantling of the social infrastructure that used to bind us together. Don't get me wrong, I'm a mad fan of change and progress. But we only need to look at the inception and rise of secular churches to realise that society knows it's lost something too.

That's right, secular churches. Sounds like a paradox, right? These are gatherings for people who want a church-like community but without all the God stuff. It's a recognition that people need community, support, help. It's a recognition that we are forced, by culture or circumstance in the West, to live our lives alone, to take care of ourselves and dig our way out of our own problems.

This lays the groundwork for an isolationist view of other people.

---

[14] https://www.mentalhelp.net/articles/facebook-and-mental-health-is-social-media-hurting-or-helping/
[15] https://www.psychologytoday.com/blog/nurturing-self-compassion/201703/mental-health-and-the-effects-social-media

How we're trained to look after ourselves

At the same time, we seem to have exponentially increased our eagerness to live by dopamine – and don't the PR people and advertisers know it! Dopamine is a neurotransmitter in the brain – we talked about it in Chapter 1. It's one of those primal mechanisms that we still have even though we don't have immediate physical threats from which we need to flee, or which we need to fight. Dopamine is linked to reward and anticipation of pleasure. If we were in a different setting, the anticipation of a big kill to feed the whole family would trigger the dopamine. What this does is flood our brain with the stuff it needs to focus on the goal – and only that. It shuts down all "non-essential services" in the body so it can solely fixate on the reward. That's why anticipation makes our heart race and we feel little butterflies in our stomachs – that's the dopamine flooding our system with adrenaline so that we're ready to act.

The adrenaline means our bodies are ready to act too– our muscles, joints, hearing, eyesight, lungs all get geared up to execute the hunt.

As modern people, dopamine has the exact same effect. Except we're not hunting to feed the family, we just saw the Macca's drive-through. Or we're about to level up in our favorite game, or we got to a cliff hanger on the latest series we're binge watching on Netflix. But dopamine is working the same way in us, even now. We see something we want, and we will go hunt for it.

Advertisers know this and so do the people that run TV stations and streaming services. Everything in our culture is geared towards a dopamine fix. That's the thing that will keep us watching, keep us buying, keep us playing, keep us sharing, keep us up-sizing, keep us hungry.

Without us even being aware of it, our instincts are supporting, and driving, our isolationist foundations. Because we are individuals, with individual phones and TVs and computers, the world is marketing to *me*. And me *alone*. And they are tapping into *my* dopamine. So, when I see something I want, I can chase it. I don't have to ask anyone. I don't have to think about it. Most of the time, money doesn't even change hands – it's just three clicks away. And since this is the way we live, a cycle of social individuality feeds a self-serve attitude, which feeds social individuality and so on and so on. It creates a social, mental, technological and emotional barrier around us all. It creates mental pathways that are so used to this behavior, that it becomes difficult to see beyond it. All our instincts are trained now on taking care of ourselves. The social and familial frameworks that would train us to do otherwise are largely gone. And thanks to our primal instincts, our own brains and bodies are focusing on ourselves and not others.

Without a significant "trip-wire" to stop our instincts, it means, as products of our culture and environment, caring for others doesn't seem to come naturally to us. And so, the Proposition seems further and further out of reach.

By contrast, Paul tells us to carry each other's burdens and so fulfill the law of Christ (Galatians 6:2). The context of this exhortation is, on the one hand watching that the sins of our brothers and sisters don't lead us into temptation, but on the other, carrying each other's burdens. We can't separate ourselves from everyone because they are sinners (we all are!). Paul exhorts us to *stay close*.

However, this is not friendship as the world understands it. Our society tends to act as if there are only two types of friendships, besties and Facebook acquaintances. There is nothing in between. You can't be besties with all your acquaintances, so you deliberately keep them in the shallow end of the friend pool.

With our church community this becomes even harder. We need to be welcoming, we need to be familiar, we need to connect and engage, and we need to be friends. So, is the "ideal" picture reasonable? We are exhorted to bear with each other in love and unity (Colossians 3:12-14), and Proverbs is jam-packed with the wisdom of friendship (e.g. Proverbs 18:24). Scripture tells us to build each other up and encourage each other (1 Thessalonians 5:11), and we are to love each other as brothers and sisters (Hebrews 13:1). But we can't be besties with 50, 100, 600 or 1000 church members, and we owe them far more than just being acquaintances? The "real" picture is completely understandable, but it's not the biblical ideal for us as believers. So, what do we do?

For starters, we need to re-assess how relationships happen, so we can distinguish different types of relationships. Then we will look at what the Bible says about how we should interact – most notably in hospitality and in love.

How do relationships happen?

I love *The King and I*. Deborah Kerr as a 19th century governess singing "Getting to know you" to all of Yul Brynner's (well, King Mongkut of Siam's) ker-jillion children has that comforting nostalgic quality that makes me feel all warm and fuzzy inside. But the sentiment is that it's the start of building a relationship. Getting to know each other is going to take time. These days I'm Facebook friends with people with just a click of the mouse. Real friendship takes more. Outlined below are just some of the platforms on which real friendship is built, and what the resulting "pillars" of close friendship are.

What is Friendship built on	What is the result
Time	Mutual trust
Shared experience	Reliance in adversity
Shared adversity	Mutual care
Memories	Mutual influence
Shared interests	Wanting the best for each other
Similar personalities	Open communication and self-disclosure
Common values	
Common social spheres	Ability to anticipate each other's needs

Those are the best kinds of friendship. This kind of real friendship is costly though. It costs time and energy and emotional effort. That's why, in our world, we put up barriers between "categories" of friends. There are those we are willing to spend time with and those we're not willing to spend time with. There are those we are willing to expend our energies on and those we aren't.

Most people in our landscape though are acquaintances. So, let's now look at them. What makes someone an acquaintance?

What are acquaintances built on	But what is missing?
A loose community connection	Self-disclosure is only one way
Mutual acquaintances	Communication generally shallow
Geographic proximity	Wouldn't go to them in a crisis
Same club/team etc.	Wouldn't expect favors
	Wouldn't expect them to advocate for you
	Generally, wouldn't spend time with, or for, each other

For most of us, this is the end of the pool we swim in with most people – including the people at our churches. We might spend time with people from church, but not nearly as much as with a real friend. There may be shared experiences but probably only within the church context. There would probably be common values based on our shared beliefs, but generally not shared interests and not even common social spheres – churches are full of diverse people who otherwise we would probably not be friends with.

But this is not exactly the picture we see in the Bible. In the Bible, outside of Jesus presenting a picture of togetherness and community with his followers, we see the early church meeting daily and sharing everything (Acts 2). And the apostles teach us to stay strong in our fellowship, to love each other and help each other along:

"And let us consider how we may spur one another on toward love and good deeds, not giving up meeting together, as some are in the habit of doing, but encouraging one another—and all the more as you see the Day approaching." Hebrews 10:24-25

The race we are running, the journey we are on, is clearly meant to happen as a group. We are not meant to try this on our own. In fact, the implication here is that if we stop meeting together, we'll be lacking in the love and good deeds department. Not because we're bad people, but because we're failing to be part of our church community, and so failing to live out our roles of encouraging others. We *need* each other.

Nobody knows for sure where the proverb "It takes a village to raise a child" comes from (thanks Wikipedia). It could be African. The idea, though, is that nobody can raise a child on their own. There must be help and input and support from a whole variety of sources whether it be family, friends, neighbors, teachers and so on – in essence a whole "village" of people. We are like these children. We are all new creations in Christ. We need our village to help raise us up well – we need people around us.

One proverb which is definitely African (I know because I googled it) is "If you want to go fast, go alone. If you want to go far, go together."

If we try to go fast, we could be successful for a while, but alone, we are doomed to supping the dregs of the Christian life. Going together means we will go further than we possibly could by ourselves.

But the world wants us to go fast, and go alone. Everything in life is geared towards this exact scenario. There are real friends. There are acquaintances. And there's nothing in between but barriers between categories. There has to be a 'third way', a way that the world doesn't know.

A New Kind of Friendship

Previously we looked at how real friendships are built and how acquaintances form. Here's a quick look at Christian friendship – how its formed and what it results in.

How do we engage	What do we want
Common beliefs	A basis of trust
Same church	Reliance in times of adversity
Same congregation	Pastorally care for each other
Ministry partnership	Influence and encourage
Serving (e.g. on teams and rosters together)	Rebuke and correct in love
	Wanting the best for them
	Meaningful communication
	Have the ability to anticipate needs

How we engage looks like how acquaintances are formed. And yet the relationships that form are characterized in a way that looks more like the real friendship list. This seems a strange truth to hold in tension.

How do you jump from acquaintance to real friend? Jesus. He is the reason we come together. He is the reason we know each other at all. He is the reason I am writing this book. And he is the reason you're reading it. If it weren't for him, none of us would be connected at all. He is the bridge from acquaintance to real friendship and he is the reason for it. He also showed us why we should do it and how we do it. So, from here, we're going to look at three key things to consider when we're approaching the people in our churches.

Hospitality (no, really)

Before all the guys switch off at this point, I don't mean entertaining. That is not the essence or point of hospitality. Hospitality is opening your life and your home. Hospitality is sharing yourself with people. And not just with the people you like – with everyone. In the New Testament, "hospitality" is the translation for *philoxenos*. It means "loving strangers" or "being a friend of strangers".

1 Peter 4:9 exhorts us to practice hospitality without grumbling. What's interesting is that this exhortation is sandwiched between verse 8 which is about loving each other deeply, and verse 10 which is about using our gifts to serve each other. The implication is that hospitality is closely linked to loving each other and using our gifts to serve each other – and mutual service is a means of deepening any relationship. In this way, relationships become self-deepening.

3 John 1:8 talks about offering hospitality as a means of working together for the truth of the gospel. Hospitality is even a qualification of a deacon or elder in 1 Timothy 3:2 and Titus 1:8. Hospitality is *that* important. Why might that be?

We are all strangers together and what binds us is Jesus. What will continue to help bind us to Jesus is each other. This means fellowship. Historically, and now, the best fellowship is had in informal settings – in our homes, over meals, through conversation, through sharing.

Truly loving each other as strangers means knowing what is going on in each other's lives – and not just knowing it but taking an interest in it.

We can 'know' what's going on in people's lives from Facebook – the bit they want to show us. But that's just head knowledge. We can know things about a person without actually *knowing* the person. Taking an *interest* in someone means we are caring about them and their life, and not just knowing about it.

To know and take an interest, we need to interact with people beyond their Facebook feed and a few pleasantries on Sunday (although both are useful!). We have an array of opportunities to be involved with each other. We can be more open-minded about what hospitality means, knowing that it doesn't mean "entertaining". If it means loving strangers, we can be in Bible study groups together, we can go to activities and events together, we can text and email. Every so often we can meet up for a chat and a coffee to ask how things are going, and to pray for each other. We can also hang out after church, or play date our kids together, or catch each other for a post-lawnmowing drink together on the weekend. During these times of fellowship and hospitality, we'll be involved in each other's lives. We'll know what to pray for each other, we'll know how to support each other.

Hospitality is an attitude. It's living openly and with a generosity of spirit. As an introvert that scares me a little, but in action, we do as much or as little as we can handle. The attitude is the important thing. How we view each other considering Jesus is the key.

We don't have to be besties in the worldly sense. We don't have to exhaust our time or give emotional energy we don't have or talk only of serious weighty issues. It's not about going out together constantly or talking every day or hosting parties. This third-way friendship is focused on each other via a focus on Christ – because we aren't trying to be best friends. We are trying to get each other closer to the cross.

The highest form of love

Love gets a bad rap these days as a feeling that comes and goes and waxes and wanes. But God commanded us to love each other, and Jesus reiterated this command as an action:

Jesus said, *"Love* [agapseis] *the Lord your God with all your heart and with all your soul and with all your mind. This is the first and greatest commandment. And a second is like it: Love* [agapseis] *your neighbor as yourself."* (Matthew 22:37-39)

The word *agapseis* is a verb ("you will love"), which means it's something we do. That doesn't mean we *feel* love for everyone, it means we love them through our actions. It means that when we text to check in, or send a message to ask for prayer points, or have pizza delivered on a night you know they're working flat out, or send a postcard just to say "thinking of you", or Skype someone who's away on long-distance placement… it's not because we're trying to be fake besties; it's because we love them and we care about their standing before God and the journey that they (and all of us!) are on.

If we love God above all else, and therefore love others as ourselves, we should care what happens to them. 1 John 3:16 says *"this is how we know what love* [agapēn] *is: Jesus laid down his life for us. And we ought to lay down our lives for our brothers and sisters." This* is how we know what agape is – from Jesus. *And we ought to* treat our brothers and sisters with this kind of love also. We are all sheep and even though we know the sound of our master's voice, we are prone to wander. Lone sheep are vulnerable to wolves. If we love each other with the love that Jesus showed for us, then we will aware of that vulnerability and care about it. We will go and find those who are vulnerable, we will stick together, and we will walk together.

Love the people the same

In Matthew 11:19 Jesus is accused of being a friend of sinners. "*The Son of Man came eating and drinking, and they say, 'Here is a glutton and a drunkard, a friend* [philos] *of tax collectors and sinners.*'"

The word is *philos* – it's a friend but someone dearly loved and trusted. It's *more* than acquaintance. In John 15:12-15 we see Jesus explaining this a bit more.

"*My command is this: Love each other as I have loved you. Greater love has no one than this: to lay down one's life for one's friends* [philōn]. *You are my friends* [philoi] *if you do what I command. I no longer call you servants, because a servant does not know his master's business. Instead, I have called you friends* [philous], *for everything that I learned from my Father I have made known to you.*"

Jesus here has described what friends look like. From Matthew 11:19 we can see from the outside looking in, Jesus' enemies accused him of treating sinners in the exact same way. What they see as shameful, we see as something beautiful. Jesus loved people the same.

Now here's a confronting question – are we like Jesus? Can we honestly say that we love the people we like, the same as the people we don't like that much? I don't mean that we're horrid to people, or rude, or are elitist or chauvinist or anything like that. But we are a diverse collection of strangers in church who otherwise would not know each other. As we see in the last table above, our connection is minimal and is largely based in Jesus. Our connection looks more like "acquaintances". But look again at the right side of the table. If we know people in our churches as acquaintances, do we still treat them like that? Or do we make the effort to treat them as dearly loved friends as Jesus modeled?

This is not easy. We may have little in common, we may have few (if any) shared interests, we may speak differently, dress differently, have a different sense of humor and all that. In the world that would be a reason to not bother. We are different to the world though – or at least we should be. This collection of people is our family. Whether we know them or not, once we are bonded together in Christ, we are family. That's why Christians were always "brothers" and "sisters" to each other. We are co-heirs to God's kingdom. This is how Jesus describes his followers. In Mark 3:34-35, Jesus' mother and brothers come looking for him:

"Then he looked at those seated in a circle around him and said, 'Here are my mother and my brothers! Whoever does God's will is my brother and sister and mother.'"

Now we don't know who was seated in this circle with Jesus – but it could have included Peter, who Jesus knew would deny him three times. It could have included Judas, who Jesus knew would betray him. It may also have included a guy who told bad jokes, a woman who laughed nervously at inappropriate moments, a man who went on a bit, and a guy with bad breath. Just because we see them in the Bible doesn't mean they were practically perfect in every way. We have to assume that being a bit annoying has been a stock pillar of humanity since the fall.

Whoever they were, Jesus expressly says that they are his family. And what does family have that a random collection of people don't have? Their bond means they tolerate difference and diversity. There is reason to weather storms together. There is reason to mend broken relationships and heal hurts. They have a sense of responsibility to each other.

They say you can't pick your family. That's right. You can't. And neither can we. God placed us where we are. He didn't place us somewhere to simply hang out with the people like us. He didn't make us a club. Just like Jesus didn't tell the disciples in Matthew 28 to go and make disciples of all nations, except the ones who aren't really like you.

God brought us into his family.

We treat our brothers and sisters as family.

Attitude is everything

Ecclesiastes 4:9-12 says

> *"Two are better than one,*
> *because they have a good return for their labor:*
> *If either of them falls down,*
> *one can help the other up.*
> *But pity anyone who falls*
> *and has no one to help them up.*
> *Also, if two lie down together, they will keep warm.*
> *But how can one keep warm alone?*
> *Though one may be overpowered,*
> *two can defend themselves.*
> *A cord of three strands is not quickly broken."*

It's quite a romantic picture of faithful togetherness. You'll usually find that last bit on a Christian cat poster or inspirational Facebook meme. What is wonderful about this though is togetherness is just *wise*. It's just *better*. Work is more productive, basic necessities of life are more easily obtained, there's defense and support in adversity. But it's quite abstract. We can nod and sigh and feel all warm and fuzzy but how easy is this in practice? Particularly in a world that prizes individuality and forces isolationism.

In Mark 2:1-12 there's a wonderful story of Jesus at Capernaum. When people heard he was there, they flocked to him, such that you couldn't get anywhere near him.

"Some men came, bringing to him a paralyzed man, carried by four of them. Since they could not get him to Jesus because of the crowd, they made an opening in the roof above Jesus by digging through it and then lowered *the mat the man was lying on. When Jesus saw their faith, he said to the paralyzed man, 'Son, your sins are forgiven.'"* (Mark 2:3-5)

Some men, and the paralyzed man was carried by four of them – which means there was more than four. A whole group of people brought one of their number to Jesus. The paralyzed man presumably had no other options open to him and he certainly wasn't going to get there of his own accord, so the friends brought him. So desperate were they to get their friend in front of Jesus that they went to the roof – a complete stranger's roof – and dug a hole through it. Isn't that a criminal act? Vandalism at the very least. The Old Testament isn't too specific on digging holes in people's rooves but Exodus 22 makes clear that property rights are taken seriously and recompense is expected as a matter of civil and religious law.

Such is their faith that they carry and accompany a friend to get him to Jesus. Such is their faith that they are not to be stopped at huge crowds. Such is their faith that they will commit petty crime to get him seen by the Messiah. And their efforts are rewarded. The man's sins are forgiven (and then his body is healed) – not because of the paralyzed man's faith, but because of his friend's faith.

That's a cord of three strands.

Is this how we behave with the people in our church? Would we do anything to get them in front of Jesus? Because in the Bible, in Jesus' world, that's what friendship looks like.

Like hospitality, this is all about attitude. We can do this kind of thing begrudgingly and eye-rollingly. Or we can just have an attitude that "this is what we do". When we have that kind of attitude, nothing is a hassle. We might have appropriate boundaries and things, but basically, this is how the village operates. We're a family. We're a village, bringing each other up. So, this is just what we do. And as much as we do it for others, so they do it for us. And that, my friends, is a pretty amazing outworking of Jesus' teaching.

Is it actually possible?

The short answer is yes but not all the time. Yes, but very brokenly. We are, after all, human. We have good days, we have bad days. We have days where we just feel a bit "meh". We have days where the church, people, life, is just too much.

Culture and society also seem to be working against us, as are our own bodies. Sometimes our own temperament, character and personality make it harder. Sometimes we conflate these things and we shouldn't – but they are linked. Temperament is someone's nature. Character is made up of, and is a product of, our values and beliefs. Personality is the outworking of our temperament and character.

When I think of "temperament" I usually think of it as an inclination. Like when you meet someone with an artistic bent, or an excitable nature. When I think of "character" I think of someone's moral fiber (or their lack of it), their backbone, their strength. When I think of "personality" I think of those awesome time-wasting tests on Facebook. It is so important to me to know which Avenger I would be, or which color or which Harry Potter character (Thor, green and Hermione Granger. In the interests of research, I did all three).

While this is pretty silly it serves to show the difference. Temperament is our natural genetic disposition. Our temperament + learned habits make our character. This means our character is shaped by our natural tendencies (temperament) as well as our observation and experience (learned habits). Personality is the outworking of this. It's what people see. Our personality is made up of Character + Behavior.

An example of types of temperament is useful to help us visualize this a bit. There are four types of temperament that Hippocrates used in the 4th century BC that are still doing the rounds today:

1. Sanguine (optimistic, active and social);
2. Choleric (short-tempered, fast or irritable);
3. Melancholic (analytical, wise and quiet); and
4. Phlegmatic (relaxed and peaceful).

Most of us are a mix of these though. So, your temperament and your learned habits (for example, how you react to conflict) make your character. This is the bit that people don't see. If we imagine this as a duck on a pond, character would be the bit below the waterline.

Your character and your behavior make your personality. This is the rest of the duck.

We can work to overcome our personality even when it doesn't yet fit our temperament. For example, with me being an introvert, I would far rather hide in a dark room with a good book than deal with the world's problems. That's what you might call the melancholic bit of my temperament. I know I am also quite excitable, big picture rather than detail, emotional rather than intellectual, so that adds a sanguine element to my temperament.

These are my genetic traits. These are mixed with my learned habits that I've picked up since I was young – everything from being scared of bees to enjoying the company of older familial men because I grew up close to my big brother.

Character informs behavior. Our behavior will not change if we think that character is fixed. But learned habits can be unlearned, and they can shift with new experiences.

I know that my learned habits are being informed by the gospel. I am learning, and I am actively trying, to move my morals and values, more and more each day, to reflect those of God. Even if my temperament is fixed, my learned habits can change with God's help.

And if my learned habits can change, my character can change, which then means my personality and behavior will change. I am hoping you are starting to see how this is reflected in scripture. In James 3 we see a particular fixation with taming the tongue. Seems OK, we might think. Not being mean and saying nasty things is very important. But look again:

With the tongue we praise our Lord and Father, and with it we curse human beings, who have been made in God's likeness. Out of the same mouth come praise and cursing. My brothers and sisters, this should not be. Can both fresh water and salt water flow from the same spring? My brothers and sisters, can a fig tree bear olives, or a grapevine bear figs? Neither can a salt spring produce fresh water. (James 3:9-12)

What we *say* is evidence of what is happening in our *heart*. This is not just about watching what we say. This is about watching how we behave because this gives us a clearer picture of where our character is.

We've gone into this in some detail, but consider this – can we really bear the burdens of our fellow brothers and sisters unless we have looked into our hearts and been able to see what is natural instinct, what is learned behavior, and most importantly, what should be unlearned?

Mini-Challenge
What do you think your temperament is? How do you
see that shaping your character and personality?
What core morals, values and beliefs underpin your character?
How do you see these two elements playing out in
your personality – what is it that people see?
What new behaviors do you think you might need to learn or sharpen?

How do we move towards the biblical picture?

You might have reached this point and thought "Wow, I'm so depressed right now. Everything is against us." So, is the ideal picture reasonable?

As the community of believers, as God's family, we lift each other up again. In Christ, we are joined together and rise to become a holy temple in the Lord (Eph 2:21). It's a lovely image – but is it realistic? Jesus' burden is light, but sometimes we feel like the burdens of our brothers and sisters are heavy.

We are not used to carrying that kind of load. We are a product of our culture. We have enough trouble carrying our own load, let alone anyone else's.

Here's the wonderful thing though. We're not built by our culture, we're only influenced by it. Deeply influenced, granted, but only influenced all the same. It's good to be aware of it, but not bound by it. Particularly since we are supposed to be different from the world, this is one of the core ways we break free of all that. And I think we all know that we want to break free. Even the people in *secular* churches know that.

God built us, and he built us to be in relationship with him and with each other. We have these pieces in front of us – culture, our own brains and bodies, our temperament, character and behavior. We also have God. And the Holy Spirit who was sent to help us on this journey.

So don't panic. We have God. And, we're all in this together right?

Reduce the size of the problem

One of the things that can get us off to a rocky start when dealing with something that doesn't come naturally to us, is working out exactly what the problem is, and how big it is.

To quote Galatians 6:2 again, Paul said *"carry each other's burdens, and in this way you will fulfill the law of Christ."* The law of Christ was clarified by Jesus himself. When asked by one of the Pharisees Jesus replied: *"'Love the Lord your God with all your heart and with all your soul and with all your mind.' This is the first and greatest commandment. And* the second is like it: 'Love your neighbor as yourself.' All the Law and the Prophets hang on these two commandments." (Matthew 22:37-40)

On this basis, as Christians, we listen to others' fears and woes, panics and pains, and emotional anguish. We hear our brothers and sisters in Christ weep and cry out to God, and we try to help and support them. We pray and we pray again. We hold their hands and walk with them as best we can. "I must help them", we think. "I need to give them time and energy and investment. To love my neighbor as myself, I have to give them everything."

There are people in your Bible study group, people in your congregation, your friends, your kids – all of them need care. Suddenly *we* are so burdened we can't think straight.

Is this what Paul intended? Is this what Jesus expected when he told us to love our neighbor as ourselves? I don't think it is. I think we've over-estimated the issue. We've made it bigger and scarier than it should be.

Which means we must be doing it wrong.

Does "burden" mean what we think it means?

The Oxford English Dictionary defines 'burden' as "a load, typically a heavy one". Think trying to carry heavy bags of shopping, or moving furniture, or struggling under the weight of suitcases. But in Galatians 6:2 *barē*/βαρη (from βαρος, burden) is a weight, but of personal significance. So the passage does call us to bear each other's 'weight' – but in a *non-physical* sense.

In Matthew 11:28 when Jesus says "*come to me all you who are weary and burdened*", he uses the word *pephortismenoi*/πεφορτισμένοι, from *phortizó*/φορτίζω, which means "loaded up to the point of being weighed down" – think those suitcases again. Then in verses 29-30 he calls us to take up his yoke for his burden is light. Here, the word for burden is *phortion*/φορτίον, which is a personal, non-transferrable load, like your own purse or suitcase that you can carry on your own.

So, while remembering we can take our burdens (*pephortismenoi*) to Jesus because his burden (*phortion*) is light, how do we bear each other's burdens (*barē*)?

What does this tell us? Firstly, there are many different kinds of burdens. The three mentioned here are not the only words used in the Greek New Testament. This difference can give us pause. We can step back and take a moment to just look at what kind of 'burden' it is — not all of them will be heavy burdens, so we need not assume that all of them are.

Secondly, we need to balance bearing each other's burdens with loving others as ourselves. When I feel my own burdens, they are heavy. But when I love myself it doesn't feel burdensome at all. Don't mishear me here. We have a whole chapter ahead about loving ourselves so please don't think this is a bad thing! The point here is that Jesus commanded us to *love*. We are to bear each other's burdens to fulfill the law of Christ. The law of Christ is loving God, and loving our neighbor as ourselves (Mark 12:29-31). Could it be that we feel overwhelmed because we are focusing on the wrong thing? We are thinking too much about burdens and not enough about love?

We may think that loving others *equals* bearing their burdens, but this is not necessarily the case. What might it look like if we loved them, rather than getting caught up in the burden itself? Remember "love" is a "doing word". Loving might look like:

- Praying for them
- Reading the Bible together
- Short visits
- Text check-ins
- Meals

- Babysitting
- Transport assistance
- Going with them to an appointment for moral support
- A card in the mail
- A care package or a small gift

The options are endless. But two things can really maximize the impact of this:

What is your personal load capacity? Some people have more capacity than others. Our capacity is a resource, and we need to use it wisely. We are stewards of our money. We try not to spend more than we have. The same needs to be true of our capacity to bear our Christian brothers and sisters' burdens.

Agree with the person what your support is going to look like. With an awareness of our load capacity, we can agree with the person about what we are going to do to support them. This is not meant to be an unfeeling transaction, but a mutual agreement in love. For example, if your load capacity is such that you feel you can manage a weekly visit, then that's what you can promise. If further need is there, you can seek assistance from others to share the load. If we communicate this openly, then expectations are appropriate and it amplifies the honoring and loving of the person as we seek to bear their burdens as a body of believers. This is particularly important if you have a "jump in and save" instinct. It is also important if someone wants to place more of a load on you than you are able to carry.

This helps practically to manage the boundaries, but what about when we feel people's load very heavily?

What do I do with the load?

God made us to be emotional beings. This makes us beautiful and wonderful, and also fragile and vulnerable. That's why Jesus told us to go to him when we are weary and weighed down. It's something we know in our heads but can forget in our hearts. It can come down to a simple question: do we believe that prayer works?

Here's the intellectual proposition – if we truly believe that God is sovereign, and we truly believe that prayer works, then when we cast our cares on Him, we will feel the burden lifted.

Do you feel like that?

That's not meant as an accusation. It's a real and genuine question because I think for a lot of us, it's not how we feel. Those of us who are more emotionally inclined can really struggle with this. I think it's because we struggle with certainty. Did God really hear? Was the burden lifted? What are my emotions telling me? What is my brain telling me?

With respect to devotional life C. S. Lewis said in *Miracles* that *"One moment even of feeble contrition or blurred thankfulness will, at least in some degree, head us off from the abyss of abstraction."* I think this sentiment holds true for casting our cares on God as well. We place enormous pressure on 'feeling' clear of whatever is happening. We like to move swiftly from problem to solution. Staying in the mess and slowly working our way through it can make us feel uncomfortable. This can be problematic. Dealing with burdens is rarely that simple, and if we try and make it that simple, it is rarely a healthy thing to do.

What is a stunning truth though is that we have a relationship with God. That means we are enabled to have an ongoing conversation with him. For example, when we take our worries to our friends, we have deep conversations. The problem is not removed straight away and we might feel better temporarily, but often it takes a few good conversations to start feeling freed of the emotional burdens. In the same way, when we are praying and casting our cares on God, even a moment of jumbled emotional words will be heard by him. And this can be enough to head us off from the kind of feeling of over-burden that stops us in our tracks. But we must talk to him again and again as we work through those burdens. And because he is sovereign, we can believe that he has heard and that he is active.

Third Way Christian Friendship

The third way of friendship – the Christian way of friendship – has exceptional clarity, because it is rooted in Christ. Christ gives our friendships boundaries and purposes that are clearly seen in Scripture, which repeatedly talks about love and unity and mutual encouragement. He also gives it focus – a focus on him which gives the strongest kind of infrastructure to our relationships. He is the reason we know each other. He is the reason we draw closer to each other. He is the reason we can be involved with each other, ask each other the right questions and show love through our actions.

Being Christ-focused doesn't mean no small talk (let's face it, what's happening on the latest reality TV show is always going to be super important), but we can ask each other "How are you going?" and mean it. We can ask "How is your spiritual life?" and genuinely want to know so we can help support each other. We can ask "What can I pray for you?" because we really are interested and we truly want to talk to God on each other's behalf.

As his disciples, we can't sit on the sidelines by ourselves. We are commanded to love each other. We bear our burdens together as we live out our lives as Christians in this world, looking forward to heaven. The best kind of friendship is wanting the absolute best for the other person. That's why the friends took the paralyzed man to Jesus.

This is who we are. It's what we do. And if you are in a place where this is not happening to you, for you or around you, please pray. And be the answer to your own prayer – be hospitable, show love in action. Look afresh at the people God has put in your Christian family, and look to love them as Jesus has asked you to.

Chapter 8

Boasting in Jesus

> ***What I think I should be doing:***
> *I will boast in Jesus Christ and evangelize constantly*
>
> ***What I really think about what I should be doing:***
> *It's really hard to be Christian in this world*

The Proposition

The Proposition is that we will evangelize persistently and tenaciously and fearlessly. We've seen or heard of the Billy Graham crusades in the 1960s, we've learned about John Wesley and the great evangelists of the 19th century, we hear about evangelism in church on Sunday and some of us have probably done several Bible studies on it. And yet the fear of boasting in Jesus remains.

Google tells me that "boasts" is to *"talk with excessive pride and self-satisfaction about one's achievements, possessions, or abilities"*. Synonyms for "boasting" include some of my favorite words, which (I think) should be brought back into common usage:

Bragging
Bluster (sounds like an *Avengers* character)
Braggadocio (please let's start using this again)
Bravado (is this a toilet cleaner?)
Exaggeration
Swank
Gasconade (not a drink)
Grandiloquence (fancy)

As great as these words sound, what they denote is bad. We've been taught this since childhood. Either it's instilled in us by our parents as they try to teach us humility, or, more likely, we learn it from our friends as we see the consequences of bragging. Nobody wants to be your friend anymore.

So, when Paul says, *"May I never boast except in the cross of our Lord Jesus Christ, through which the world has been crucified to me, and I to the world,"* in Galatians 6:14, is this Paul being a bit of a jerk? Is this Paul saying we should exaggerate and give our witnessing to Jesus a bit of brag and bluster?

We know this is not the case. But here is where we have a tension between the world and the Bible. "Boasting" in the world is arrogance. It's about pointing attention to ourselves at the expense of other people. "Boasting" in the Bible doesn't mean exaggeration or bluster, but to take pride in something, to exult in something. And for us, this "something" is Jesus, so in taking pride in Jesus we point not to ourselves but to him.

Do you boast in Jesus? Do you boast in him to the exclusion of *all* else, as Paul is suggesting? Before we answer that, let's look more closely at what Paul is actually saying.

The Galatians were boasting in the wrong thing

For starters, let's look at the context. This whole letter to the Galatians has been a corrective to a church that has been swayed by people preaching "Repentance + Faith-Plus". Repentance we know. Faith we know. But what is "Faith-Plus"? What that means is true repentance of sins, faith in Jesus Christ PLUS circumcision. The Jewish Christians had become quite savvy in their marketing. They were preaching fear. Fear of leaving the old ways behind. Fear of the unknown. They were hedging their bets. They were following Jesus but they were keeping some of the old Jewish ways *just in case*.

"But that's not faith!" I hear you cry. Aah. True. That's why you are smarter than the Galatians. Let's not be too harsh though. Let's think about where these people were. If I told you to step on a rattle snake to avoid being bitten, I suspect you would not believe me for a second. If you did believe me, you might wear steel cap boots and thick gaters just in case. This is where the early Jewish Christians were. Following Jesus meant putting aside all the trappings and ceremonies of the Jewish religion – the very things they have been trained to do in order to be right with God. Yes, we'll repent and believe, *but just in case*, we'll do these other things as well. It's not a big deal to hedge your bets is it? It doesn't hurt anyone. If I step on a rattle snake and I'm wearing boots and gaters, that's not a problem for anyone else. If we believe in Jesus but keep bits of the old ways, it's not a deal breaker.

The problem is that it *is* a deal breaker. The problem is that this doctrine teaches that the *cross is not enough*. This is the precipice we walk when we put too much reliance in the wrong things. Any simple thing can become "works" if we give them too much power. Things we do to be obedient and faithful, become works if we let them. Like reading the Bible. It's where we started this book. That's a good thing, a worthy thing, but not as a special ritual. We do it frequently because we want to meet Jesus in its pages and allow the Word to do its work in us. We don't do it because it will get our go-to-heaven ticket stamped, like it's a frequent flyer program or something.

When we do that, it takes a little bit of our reliance away from the cross, and onto something else. And that's a problem for us. Because left un-checked, we end up where the Galatians were.

They were boasting in the wrong thing for the wrong reasons

Paul also accuses the teachers of this Faith-Plus doctrine of doing it to avoid persecution. At the time this letter was written (in the late 40s or early 50s AD), being Jewish was a "legitimate religion" in the Roman Empire. That meant that is was recognized by the Romans and it was legal to practice that religion. Illegitimate religions were those ones that were not recognized by the Romans because they were thought to be a threat of some kind to the Roman status quo. These religions were met with strong penalties, and the Romans did not muck about with their penalties.

Christianity was not at that point a separate religion to Judaism. It was seen as a sect or sub-set of it. Jesus had fulfilled the Law and the prophets, not abolished them. He had taken Judaism to its next level and natural, fore-ordained conclusion. The fact that most Jews didn't believe that meant that followers of Jesus were seen as just some crazy off-shoot heretics – but not yet part of a separate religion.

As part of the Jewish religion, followers of Christ were technically still within the bounds of a legitimate religion and not subject to persecution. If they were too radical and broke away, they would officially be a new religion, one that was illegitimate in the eyes of the Romans. If the Christians were an illegitimate religion, the Romans would start hounding and persecuting them.

Interesting history facts, aren't they? It means that on a purely logistical front, doing Jewish rituals along with your Christian beliefs meant you still looked like a Jew. That would keep you clear of the Romans and their persecution. It was essentially being Jewish with a spritz of Christianity for the sake of avoiding trouble, saving face and being "in" with the "in-est" crowd there was at that time.

Feeling like you have to fit in

Let's go back a bit and follow this through. In verse 12 Paul says that *"those* [being those who are all-for adding Jewish rites] *who want to impress people by means of the flesh* [that is, make an outward show] *are trying to compel you to be circumcised"*. How do you compel someone to be circumcised? We're not talking physical violence here – that's not what Paul is alluding to. How do you feel compelled to do something?

Think about that for a moment. What makes you feel compelled to do something?

The Galatians were facing fear and uncertainty with the Romans and the broader Jewish community (which was still *their* community). They were being shamed into it. The Jewish leaders had sowed enough doubt for the Galatians to go from fear, over the compulsion threshold, to action. The Judaisers were compelling them by appealing to their baser emotions and survival instincts.

We see this in our day and age. Every time there is an election, usually there is at least one candidate that tries to use fear to make us vote for them. They sow the seeds of doubt that there is a threat to our safety, to our jobs, our homes and our money. They sow the seeds of fear. You end up with that uncomfortable feeling in your stomach and anxiety about what you could lose. This is what the Galatians faced.

And oh! The hypocrisy! Paul goes on to say that this desire to impress, truly is all outward show because (verse 13) not even they follow the law! But they want the Galatians to tow the line, so they can boast in their achievements in converting them to their way of thinking. And what have they achieved? Kudos. They have followers who will do what they say. They have status and sway over these followers that other people can see. So this is nothing to do with Jesus, or the cross, or salvation. This is about those people. It's outward show to avoid trouble, and to build themselves up.

This is what they boast in. And Paul quite rightly says, if I am going to boast in anything, let it only be the cross of Jesus Christ. His statement will not keep him out of trouble. It will not make him look good. It will not build his status. But it is the *only thing* worth taking pride in.

What compels us to do anything?

Okay, you might think. I know all that. Yup. Me too. So why don't I boast in Jesus Christ? I don't know about you, but more often than not I feel more compelled to be a quiet Christian than a Christian who is crucified to the world. Why is that?

Well, there's an "in" crowd today, just like there was then. For the Galatians, it was the Romans. For us, it's called "everyone else". "Everyone else" permeates our whole lives – work, friends, Facebook contacts, people down at the shops, people we meet on the street, people on the TV and radio, people in authority and governing positions. And the current climate runs against us Christians. People don't understand us. Or, they think they understand us and they mock us. They make fun of what we believe. Some of them even hate what we believe. There are countries where being a Christian is illegal. Christians are imprisoned and persecuted. Christians in some parts of the world simply "disappear".

Here in the West, praise God, we are supremely safe by comparison. But every time we look at Facebook or turn on the TV, our senses are bombarded by stories of how what we believe is prehistoric. We hear that

Christianity is oppressive, that it hurts people. We hear that we are bigots and idiots. Me? Living in my little house with my kids just trying to get through the day without screaming or having a nervous breakdown? I have enough to worry about without the world thinking I'm a moron.

Don't get me wrong, I am not mocking our lives. Far from it. What I'm saying is we have compelling reasons to keep our voices low. It really is hard enough to go with the flow, let alone fight against the prevailing winds.

But we shouldn't be worried by that. One thing the New Testament shows us is that Christianity has never been the norm, not really. Ever since the glorious day that Jesus rose, the disciples were always swimming upstream. Christians were mocked, scorned, persecuted, tortured and killed. There were fights within the church itself, there were attacks on the church from outsiders. So, yes, it is hard to be a Christian in this world. But then again, *it always has been.*

Putting this aside then, I think there are two key elements to this puzzle. Fear and Laziness. Don't switch off here – by "laziness" I mean the science of "engagement", so stick with me for a great story. But let's start with fear.

What is it we are really afraid of?

Fear is one of the most compelling forces. The fear of going against the tide, of being outside the in-crowd. Why? Because we might look foolish. Because it will hurt us. Because we might get a bad reaction from people. Because we will be thought less of. This last one is as strong as it is insidious. It lies at the heart of some of our worst and most stubborn inactivity. It is also completely understandable, which is why it is worth dissecting.

The human ego is an interesting thing and it's not what we think. We commonly think of the ego as something that is massive in arrogant people and small in humble people. But the ego is more than that. The ego is just what we believe about ourselves, which is why is can be quite vulnerable.

If we believe lots of great things about ourselves, being thought less of is a big hit to our pride. Which hurts. For instance, for my little boy being known to be honest is really important to him. When another kid in class accuses him of telling fibs, he is inconsolable.

On the other hand, if we believe a lot of negative things about ourselves, being thought less of represents a confirmation to us of all our worst fears, which is crippling. For example, I have always worked quite hard at school and uni. My brother was the "fun one" which meant I was left with being "the pretty one", "the cool one", "the sporty one" or "the brainy one". Not that we pick our childhood personas from The Spice Girls but we all know that feeling of "who am I?" that hits us during our teen years. For me, the least terrible option was being the brainy one, but it never came naturally and I always suspected that I was a bit dumb. It is now so ingrained, that if I get poor marks on an assignment (yes, I continue to study to this day!), instead of brushing it off, I seem disproportionately upset with myself.

So, the ego is incredibly important for our motivation, which drives how we behave and the choices we make. Some might not boast in the cross for fear of being looked down on. Others might not boast in the cross for fear of a tangible proof of what we always thought about ourselves.

Here's a question. What do you think about yourself? Do you think you are smart? Funny? Vulnerable? Kind? Weak? Wise?

Here's the next question: What does my self-perception matter? Would it matter if other people thought the same, or thought differently? What's the *worst* that could happen?

These questions are useful because they help us start developing some tools to overcome the things that stop us living to our full potential.

Fear is habit forming. Living to avoid fear leads you to a comfort zone. Once you're in the comfort zone, it becomes harder and harder to break out. So changing takes work.

The answer to the second question is particularly difficult to work through in my opinion, because the tenor of the answer is different depending on the attitude you have cultivated. The diagrams below show what I mean.

What I tell myself	I'm stupid.
What happens when I boast in Jesus:	They think I'm stupid.
What that does:	It confirms my worst fears about myself.
What I tell myself:	OPTION 1 – Instinctive response I knew it. They think I'm stupid, they'll tell me I'm stupid, they'll think less of me, they'll tell others I'm stupid, they won't just think I'm stupid, they'll *know* I'm stupid. OPTION 2 – The response to cultivate Huh. Turns out I might be stupid after all. I reckon I'm doing okay for a stupid person. OR Huh. They might think I'm stupid but only according to them. Jesus doesn't think I'm stupid. I'm doing what he told me.

What I tell myself	I'm amazing and awesome.
What happens when I boast in Jesus:	They think I'm stupid.
What that does:	That really hurts.
What I tell myself:	OPTION 1 – Instinctive response This will hurt my reputation, I will lose credibility, they'll think I'm fake and they won't believe me anymore. OPTION 2 – The response to cultivate Well, they just found out something new about me. Let's see how they deal with this! OR So I lost a little face. What's a bit of that when Jesus suffered on the cross?

This is not easy to process. And the examples above are overly simplistic. But you can see that the *big difference* in boasting or not boasting, between acting or not acting, is *how we speak to ourselves*. So, if, in prayer and diligence, we can cultivate a different self-talk, we can train ourselves to get over this. We can develop a better learned behavior. It will never be natural, it will be learned. But we can do it if we are aware of it.

Another good way of pushing this further is to have a conversation with yourself that runs along these lines:

ME: They'll think less of me.
ALSO ME: And how bad would that be?
ME: They'll think I'm stupid.
ALSO ME: And how bad would that be?
ME: It might mean I really am stupid.
ALSO ME: And how bad would that be?

ME: It might mean I am on the "out" with this group.
ALSO ME: And how bad would that be?
ME: Being outside the group feels bad.
ALSO ME: And how bad would that be?

And so it goes on… Now don't get me wrong. There might be real consequences. Painful consequences. What this self-conversation is aimed at though is pinpointing what the thing is that you fear, and then, evaluating how much that means to you, and means to you comparatively (i.e. is being in a group more valuable than being with Jesus?). It might still hurt terribly, but at least we are looking at it in its proper perspective.

This will help us answer the real questions:

What will I lose by boasting in the cross?
Is it more important than the cross?

Grappling with "laziness" or the science of engagement

Have you heard the term "slacktivism"? It's a fairly new term. It describes a slack activism. A modern phenomenon has been the moral outrage with which we encounter things (bombings in the Middle East, child soldiers, stolen child brides, mass incarceration and persecution of Christians or any people group, enormous death rates in developing countries from preventable diseases…) and yet we are not compelled to turn the outrage into action.

Generally, our human logic is that a particular cause is worthy of pursuit in and of itself. If I see an advert for Compassion or Voice of the Martyrs, I might think "That is a worthy cause because of what it seeks to do." In my brain, that makes the cause worthy of pursuit. But this is not the case. It is not the case because we might have had our awareness raised, but we haven't *engaged* with it.

Some very clever science type people have worked out that actual <u>action</u> happens when there is value alignment, not just awareness raising.[16] What this might look like is if I see an advert for Compassion that shows me a child the same age as my own. That aligns with what I value and so I will be engaged, not just a spectator.

What they also found is that public actions will reflect private beliefs and that those actions are more likely to result in deeper engagement. So again, I might want to sponsor a child because caring for children aligns with my personal values. But I might choose Compassion because it is also important to me that Jesus be known and glorified. This deepens my engagement because I feel that my beliefs are being lived out through my actions. I might feel I am being a good and faithful servant.

What is also a factor is that private acts are more commonly related to *deeper* engagement. So, I have sponsored my child, but then I start writing letters and learning about them. In the process I learn more about their family and their country and about Compassion and the work that they do. None of these are posted on Facebook, it's just the ongoing process of child sponsorship. This all happens behind closed doors. But I am learning and I am growing and my engagement is deepening. This might then lead me to a visit to my sponsor child, or a short mission trip, or becoming an ambassador for Compassion or sponsoring more children.

So the corollary effect is this:

> ➤ Awareness raising (i.e. becoming aware of an issue through ads, social media, TV etc.) and feeling moved/outraged/interested etc.

---

[16] "The Nature of Slacktivism: How the Social Observability of an Initial Act of Token Support Affects Subsequent Prosocial Action" Author(s): Kirk Kristofferson, Katherine White, and John Peloza Source: *Journal of Consumer Research*, Vol. 40, No. 6 (April 2014), pp. 1149-1166.

> The awareness raising campaign promotes values and not just actions, that align with a person's own values which moves the individual from interested observer to engaged participant (i.e. we have gotten over the compulsion threshold to action)
> Public acts reflect these private beliefs
> Private acts deepen the engagement further (which translates to further action)

Deeper engagement = more action.

Why aren't we engaged like this with the gospel? We feel like we are engaged because we believe it to be true, and yet many of us still lead quiet lives, avoiding any kind of boasting in the cross. I know some people who, working in secular workplaces, "check their Christianity at the door". I used to do this too. I know people who, when asked what they did at the weekend, think twice about saying they went to church. I also used to do this.

It's hard. There's strength in (Christian) numbers. We're outnumbered by everyone else. But if we believe that Jesus is Lord, then surely, we should and would, boast in him. We know it. We believe it. But it looks like we aren't engaged with it.

Why not?

Well, there's a big emphasis on value alignment in the clever-people-paper. We need to know what the values are so we can evaluate if they align with our personal values. Or we can align ourselves to those values because we believe they are the values that we want to have. This makes the issue personal.

People talk about Christian values a lot. They are things like grace, hope, faith, love, justice, joy, service and peace. You might recognize them because a couple of hundred years ago, parents called their children all these things. These are wonderful and beautiful values. But I wonder if for us, they are a bit conceptual. They are hard to put your arms around. They seem grand and far away – like the names of a couple of hundred years ago.

Values are a general expression of what is important to you. While "Christian values" (in the traditional or old-fashioned sense) might be things we like and believe in through a gospel lens, they might not be personal. Our values (which are also Christian, but didn't make it to the Name List a couple of hundred years ago) might be things like:

- Fairness
- Family
- Courage
- Compassion
- Curiosity
- Generosity
- Creativity
- Integrity
- Community
- Status
- Discipline

Have a think about what your values are. What is important to you?

The next step is this: What actions would express this value in your life? For example, for me, one of my values is curiosity. One of the ways that value is expressed is in my parenting. I work hard to expose my kids to things that are interesting, that are tantalizing, that need researching, that require discovery.

If you're having trouble thinking about what your values are, it's interesting to think about what the values are you dislike in people (dishonesty, small mindedness, self-righteousness, greed etc.) and then you can work out what the opposite is – these are the values you have or would like to have.

Another way of really pinning down what is integral to your identity and most personal beliefs, is to quiz yourself:

1. When were you most happy? What were you doing? Who were you with?
2. When were you most proud? Who did you share it with and how did you describe it?
3. When were you most fulfilled? What specific desire was fulfilled and how did it give your life meaning?
4. What do you want to pass on to your kids? If you could gift them any beliefs, attitudes or behaviors what would they be and why?
5. Who do you look up to and why? What values do they express that you admire?

When you've started to pin this down, it will connect back up to traditional Christian values – but it will make them seem more real. Let me show you:

I am most happy when I am larking about with my kids. I am most proud usually when my kids have gotten over some big personal milestone (like dealing with consequences or overcoming hurdles) and the first people I tell are my three best friends. I am most fulfilled when I am writing. Not necessarily Christian stuff, lots of different things, but it fulfills a desire in me to raise questions and investigate them and follow them to their conclusion. It gives my life meaning because it brings me into the thick of all the richness that life has to offer.

The main things I want to pass onto my kids are compassion, mission mindedness and a heart for justice, a work ethic, respect for people and a heart for standing up for others

I look up to assassinated presidential hopeful Bobby Kennedy for his ability to change his course of action on the basis of new facts, for his balance of dogged work ethic and close family connection, and for his unceasing efforts to change the world for the better. I look up to William Tyndale, translator of the first full English Bible in the 16th century who was exiled and executed, for his passion to see everyone have access to God's word. I love his determination, his quiet devotion and his affection for language and God's words in particular.

These values roughly translate to: family, joy, community, persistence, curiosity, compassion, justice and mission, work, passion and communication. These would all sit happily under the Christian banner. What they are not, however, is (as yet) connected to the gospel – which is the next step in our process of self-motivation.

How do we keep this about Jesus and not about us?

The danger with self-reflection is getting stuck focusing on ourselves at the expense of God. Self-reflection is important stuff though. Because if it's *us* that stops us boasting in the Lord, we need to understand what we are doing to ourselves, and then overcome it.

We know why we should boast in Jesus. Because when Jesus bled on the cross, he did it for us. It was the single most important moment in history. A single moment when the universe held its breath. That second when all of us were connected in a silent breathless moment of suffering. An instant of connection of every particle in the universe in a flash and a scream of such love and anguish that we would never be the same again.

There is an argument that says that much of the book of Revelation describes not what is to come, but what has already happened. In the letter to the churches, John describes in apocalyptic language, what happened at the cross. This is where we get a picture of the full weight of what Jesus took on our behalf.

"I watched as he opened the sixth seal. There was a great earthquake. The sun turned black like sackcloth made of goat hair, the whole moon

turned blood red, and the stars in the sky fell to earth, as figs drop from a fig tree when shaken by a strong wind. The heavens receded like a scroll being rolled up, and every mountain and island was removed from its place." (Rev 6:12-14)

This is the cup of poison drunk by Jesus. The full force and fury of God's wrath descending on the head of his son with all the burning white-hot ferocity of a million fiery suns. This was what the punishment for the sin of the world looked like. Not just a personal suffering of a horrible death, but a tsunami of blazing wrath landing on the head of one man.

This is not about us. This was never about us.

If I have my list of values in one hand and the Bible in the other, every page screams into my soul its truth and weight. When I read about Jesus seeking out the demon possessed man in the Gerasenes in Mark 5, I weep for the despairing, pathetic words of the man as he explains that his name is Legion "Because we are many" and I revel in the compassion of Christ in his treatment of him.

When I read about Jesus withdrawing alone to pray, and then appealing to his Father in the garden of Gethsemane, I am in awe of his ability to keep going, knowing what is to come.

When I read the Psalms, I glory in the richness of the text and the realness of the emotion. My heart echoes the cry of the Psalmist when he wonders "What is man that you are mindful of him?"

When I read the crucifixion accounts, I can imagine Jesus' mother watching her beautiful boy suffer. My heart breaks for her. But I also understand what Jesus is doing and my heart breaks that he went through that for me. *Who am I that you are mindful of me?*

This was never about us. It was always about him. But I live *my* life as though it was about *me*. My values are *my* values. They are based on what is important to *me*. So I need to go back to the Bible and see my values written in the pages of the gospels. I need to read the Psalms and recognize that God created me with a million different emotions and that he recognizes every single one of them. I need to read the Old Testament and feel the struggle and the hope of the Israelites, and understand what injustices break God's heart.

I believe the Bible because it is God's inspired word to us. It is the bedrock of my belief. My values are the things that have become important to me over time. When you read the Bible knowing what your values are, you will see them there. You will see your values meet their ultimate expression in Jesus. And you will engage.

We are the in-crowd

Let's get some perspective.

We are human and far from perfect. We have short memories. We forget that we are not the center of our universe. Don't worry, we all do it.

So, redressing the balance takes some self-reflection. The kind of self-reflection that's about re-directing ourselves authentically and freely to Jesus as our savior *and* our Lord.

Assess what you are afraid of losing. What is it that you hold dear that is at stake if you boast in the Lord?

Work out what your values are. I think you'll find they align back to so-called Christian values. Pick up the Bible and see your values there. See yourself there. We are aligned with the story. We are *in* the story. We are part of God's plan. So we should and will boast in the Lord.

The concept of boasting in its biblical context holds the notion of glorying – specifically glorying in oneself, hence the rendering of "boasting". Imagine if we didn't talk about boasting in the Lord but *glorying* in him. What would that look like? If we gloried in Jesus, we would hold him up for praise, we would revel in him, we would revel in his words. We would want to tell everyone about him and who he is and what he has done. It means that our outward actions would reflect our deeper convictions and private beliefs:

> How we parent
> Volunteering for charitable works
> Serving our friends and expressing love through action
> Living in community – "doing life" with people on a far deeper and more fundamental level.
> How we speak
> How we treat our resources and the world around us

So, having worked through all that, how would you glory in Jesus? Think it through again. Connect to yourself. Connect yourself to the gospel. Allow God to lead you where he wants you to go. Be still and know that he is God. He has given you the tools and knowledge to do what he wills.

Connect to yourself.

Connect yourself to the gospel.

How would you glory in Jesus?

Chapter 9
Pastorally Caring for Others

> **What I think I should be doing:**
> *I will live a life of compassion and pastorally care for others*
>
> **What generally happens:**
> *A lot less than what I think I should be doing – and feeling guilty about it. There's only so much I can do*

The Proposition

Caring for others is what Christians do, isn't it? We start charities and care for the poor and the sick and the disadvantaged. The Proposition is just this kind of picture – that now we are Christian, we should be trying to alleviate suffering in the world and in our neighborhoods.

Caring for others is something I try and teach my kids to do as a fundamental ethic but have to work hard to do myself. I'm really good at blessing myself in a thousand different ways. I buy coffee on my way to work. I decide to work at home for the day. I get my hair done because (my children tell me), it looks like the legs of up-ended spiders. I'll meet up with a friend on a whim. I decide to have that second helping of spaghetti bolognaise. I'm feeling a bit tired so I decide I'll do the washing up tomorrow instead of tonight. These are things that barely even register in my brain – I am so used to making decisions that bless myself.

God also blesses me beyond measure. He saved me. He uplifts me. He sustains me. He protects me. He provides for me. He is there in the darkest hours and he celebrates with me in my times of triumph.

A really clever guy once said that "God blesses us like I give me hot chocolate".[17] We heap hot chocolate into our mug of milk with abundance. We heap it high. Because the more chocolatey the better, right? What is incredibly wise in this saying, is the acknowledgement that God blesses us with this kind of abundance. The downside is, we also bless ourselves with this kind of abundance.

Do we bless others with the same sense of abandon?

I don't. Because surely there is only so much I can do. I only have so many hours. How much am I supposed to do? I have elderly neighbors, my Bible study group and people in my congregation who really need pastoral time. But there's also a higher rate of domestic abuse in my area and so much mortgage stress that there is increasing stress on mobile food vans. And is world hunger or even homelessness in my local area going to be even remotely alleviated on the basis of the puny amount of hours I have?

Well, let's pick this apart, because pastoral care seems to be a core biblical concept, and so it's something we clearly need to look at. There must be something in there that God wants us to see and practice. It might even be something that energizes us for the journey and makes the journey easier.

What does it mean to bless someone?

You know when someone sneezes? You say "Bless you". I was once told that sneezing was one of the first signs of the plague in the Middle

---

[17] Craig Hamilton https://matthiasmedia.com.au/search?type=product&q=craig+hamilton

Ages so if you sneezed, someone would bless you in the hopes of warding off the disease. I don't know if that's true, but I guess it relates to ye olden times when to bless someone was to pray protection over them. But then in a small school in the north of England in the 1970s some evil little toddler told me in the playground that if you said "Bless you" when someone sneezed, a fairy would die. I'm not really sure of the connection between blessing someone and a fairy dying, but I was horrified all the same.

What is blessing though? It's bandied around a lot these days. It's even a trending hashtag #blessed. I don't know if it means what people think it means. It appears as a hashtag on anything that's good. "Having the most amazing breakfast #blessed", "Hanging out with my friends #blessed", "Just got upgraded #blessed".

For the Christian, it carries so much more weight. When we say "blessed" we mean by God. It means we've been given something we didn't expect and didn't deserve. Sometimes we even describe these things as "God moments" when something unexpected and providential happens. As Christians we don't believe in coincidence. We believe in God sustaining and providing for us. God blesses us in a thousand different ways every day. Often, we don't even realize it until we look back with hindsight and are able to see how God put all the pieces in the right place so it culminated in just the way it did. But if we develop our observational skills, we notice how God blesses us in so many different ways.

Do you ever write down your prayers? It's a useful exercise – over time you'll see just how many of them are answered.

Do you keep a gratitude journal? Writing down just a couple of things every day starts to hone your blessing-observation skills. God doesn't just bless us with friends, jobs, kids and houses (whatever that looks like), he also blesses us with sunny days, and music, and the color green, and your favorite book and cheese and lie-ins on a weekend.

These are the things we need to observe. The abundance of blessing in everything around us that we normally take for granted, or don't even see because there are blessings everywhere.

I find myself doing this, and even a few days of a gratitude journal (because who can keep anything going longer than a couple of days?) is a useful self-corrective. Let me put it this way – my youngest boy is a shocker for focusing on the things he doesn't have. The cupboard is full but there's *nothing* to eat. We went to the shops and then the cinema and we had toys and treats and fun times – and yet when we stop at the grocery store on the way home to get dinner, but we didn't get a treat for him, guess who had a mega-meltdown (clue: it wasn't me). Now okay, he's 5. He's being (annoyingly) age appropriate and still learning the hard lessons about gratitude and how much is enough. But what's my excuse? If I could get my 5-year-old to act like a 30-year-old and write down all the blessings he had received that day, it would have re-adjusted his perspective. That's why I find a gratitude journal – even for a few days – a very helpful exercise to re-adjust my focus back to what God has blessed me with.

There's another side to blessing though – when we are supposed to bless the Lord. Which seems strange because how can we bless God? What can we possibly give him that he would need? Psalm 103 starts *"Praise the Lord, my soul"*. Or, as the King James and English Standard Version rendered *"Bless the Lord, O my soul."* This word "bless" in Psalm 103 is בָּרַךְ *barak*. It means to adore on bended knee. It's intensely active – like having a built-in superlative. It means we adore God with *all* of our being. So much more than praising him, we adore him with everything we are, humbly, on bended knee. God doesn't need this, but he wants it. He wants us to bless him through our praise and worship. We praise and worship him through a life of love for him – genuine sacrificial love.

We have been blessed by God in so many ways. How do we apply this blessing to others?

Blessing others like I bless myself

Doing "good" can be a poisoned chalice. We love people who do good. We want to be ethical. We love world changers. However, there is still a danger here that our pride and virtue signaling will take over our genuine intentions. At some point, we can move over the other side of the bell-curve to become sanctimonious do-gooders. Or even worse, we do good because we are supposed to and suddenly we have moved from resting in being saved by faith, to trying to save ourselves through good works.

What is the right balance?

Mark 12 gives us Jesus' definitive opinion about how we are supposed to live when asked about which of Moses' ten commandments is the most important. In response, Jesus says: *"Love the Lord your God with all your heart and with all your soul and with all your mind and with all your strength. The second is this: Love your neighbor as yourself. There is no commandment greater than these."* (Mark 12:30-31)

Love God. Love your neighbor. In that order.

He didn't just say it though, he actually lived it out. Jesus is quoted by John as saying *"I have set you an example that you should do as I have done for you."* (John 13:15) A much-used passage in the Old Testament exhorts God's people to *"Act justly, love mercy and walk humbly with your God."* (Micah 6:8) Jesus reiterates this in Matthew 23:23 saying that the hypocritical Pharisees have neglected *"justice, mercy and faithfulness."* What Jesus says here is the bumper sticker version of Micah. What is important about that is how we are to hear this. Jesus came to fulfill the law and the prophets. In the process he corrected people's focus from outward trappings (food laws, cleanliness rituals and crazy Sabbath observances) to a demeanor of the heart that is centered around obedience, a clean heart and focus on God and not a million regulations. In a few places though, Jesus specifically draws Old Testament observances into his teaching. This is one of them. While outward food rituals need to be re-interpreted with reference to the status of the heart, our attitude to others remains as strong as God's heart. The prophet Micah told the people they needed to act justly and love mercy – so did Jesus. And so must we.

So what is it that Jesus is pointing us to here? Let's look again.

In Micah, to act justly means to act in accordance with the laws and regulations and so on. The Israelites had the 10 commandments (Exodus 20:1-17) of which the most important are loving God, and loving others as we love ourselves (Mark 12:30-31 and Matthew 22:36-40) as we saw previously. As we love ourselves? We love ourselves a lot. We love our friends and family, possibly as much as we love ourselves. We can feel deep compassion for cute kids and people who look and sound like us (it's human nature to engage with people that resonate with us). Can we love people we don't like? Can we love people who are alcoholics? Gamblers? Violent people? Prisoners? People who look different and sound different, dress differently and don't have the same manners and expectations?

Jesus did. In Mark 5 we see Jesus get into a boat and go to a Gentile area (the Gerasenes) for no other purpose than to interact with a poor, pathetic demon possessed man. His name is Legion because he is possessed by so many. He lives in a cemetery and is in such demented anguish that he has clawed at his own flesh. His clothes are rags and he is mentally and emotionally unstable. He is a picture of despair and agony. For Jesus, a Jew, this man is an unclean Gentile (the Gerasenes is a Gentile area) and, in so many other ways, Jesus is made ceremonially unclean by this man – he lives among the dead, near pigs, he is dirty and covered in blood.

And yet Jesus went to him and cared for him and healed him. He took care of his spiritual needs as well as his material needs. We know this because when people came to see what had happened, *"they saw the* man who had been possessed by the legion of demons, sitting there, dressed and in his right mind." (Mark 5:15) He was calm, and he was dressed.

Then Jesus got back in the boat and left. That's it – that was the point of Jesus journey there. He went by boat to this area, healed this man, got back in the boat, and left. There was nothing else he had gone there to do. The only thing on his "to-do" list, was to care for this terrified anguished soul. He sought him out. He put Legion, a man who was unclean and so different to Jesus in every way, ahead of himself. This is his example. It's an example he specifically wanted us to see. It's not something that happened by-the-by on his way to do something else. No. This was an event that had purpose and significance in and of itself. It's something he wanted us to see very clearly.

Back to Micah. Micah says the people of God are to love mercy. Not just do it, not just like it, but *love* it. We understand mercy as having compassion on someone, particularly someone under our control. But biblical mercy has the richness of unfailing love and devotion. There's tenacity. God didn't say "have a go" at mercy, he said pursue it tenaciously because it's a heart thing. When we love people with that kind of loyalty, it's more than just giving money to cancer research (although don't get me wrong, we should totally give money to charity!), it's about forming relationships with people, it's about wanting people's lives to be better.

We can be accidental tourists in many ways. We want to do good things. Without proper prayer and wisdom though, we can fall into the trap of doing things to achieve some sense of rightness on our part. This makes those acts about us – not about other people's live being better in the long term.

The third item in Micah's statement is summarized by Jesus in Matthew as "faithfulness". A faithfulness to God means that our heart is changed, and our outward actions will reflect this humility and obedience. We do things to glorify God, not us. So doing "good stuff" or blessing others, is not about us. It's not even really about the other person. It's about glorifying God.

If we approached acts of blessing as a means of glorifying God, as acts that spring from a humble and genuine heart that seeks to reflect God through a persistent and tenacious pursuit of making someone's life better – how much more effective our actions might be! Instead of one act of "I should really do something" it might become an act that truly glorifies God and results in an unknown numbers of blessings.

Who are we supposed to bless?

Here's a side question – who are we supposed to bless? I mean, let's face it – there are people everywhere who need to be blessed. Do we focus our efforts on our local church? On our local community? On our town or region? On our country? On the world?

If we are to love our neighbors as ourselves, then it has to be everyone. But surely that's not possible! Let's weigh this up – if we love our neighbors as ourselves, it's a heart thing. If we love justice and mercy, it's a demeanor – it's a way of approaching life generally. If we have cultivated this heart and this attitude, then Galatians 6:10 makes sense:

"Therefore, as we have opportunity, let us do good to all people, especially to those who belong to the family of believers."

There are several elements in this verse that are worthy of note:

1. Let us do good to *all people*: It seems to be a universal rule, although;
2. *Especially* to believers: We have a pastoral responsibility to our brothers and sisters; but
3. *As we have opportunity:* If we have a heart for justice and mercy and compassion, we will see the opportunities and take them.

This requires more thoughtful digging so we don't misinterpret what Jesus said. "As we have opportunity" isn't a get-out clause. When we stand before the throne, I don't think "Not seeing any opportunities" is going to impress very much. We know that there are opportunities everywhere. The question is, how are we to use our discernment to choose which opportunities we act on. Only you can answer that. But I know some people who try to be proactive – for example, as a matter of habit they make an extra meal every week and then they can choose to bless someone, every week.

Some people pray and listen to where God is leading them. They ask for the opportunities God wants them to act on.

I would recommend a Pray-and-Plan approach. First, prayer. Pray for God to shape your heart. Pray for God to give you eyes to see. Pray for help from the Holy Spirit.

Second. Plan. How much time do you have? How much money do you have? This is not a trick question. Before I had children, I worked for an engineering firm 50km away from home. That meant I had money but no time. When I had children, I had more time but no money. Either situation is not bad. It's just a fact of what is possible in your landscape. What is your time/money ratio?

Pray again. Is the ratio right or do you need to re-visit it? If God is leading you to pastorally care for young adults or seniors but you have no time, are there things you can do to change your situation to make that possible? Can you work at home for a day a week so instead of commuting, you can spend an hour or so pastoring others?

Maybe it can't change. But it's worth planning, then praying, then planning and then praying again. Because this demeanor is important, so we need to make space in our lives to allow God to shape us in the way he wants.

And God even built us to do it

You know what else? We are wired to step out in love and mercy, to care for one another and bless each other . C. S. Lewis, in *Mere Christianity*, explains it as Moral Law. That is, all human beings have an innate sense of right and wrong that runs counter to nature. If the cold hard laws of the universe are true, we should not feel compelled, apparently without thinking about it, to jump into a freezing lake to save someone. This deep sense of duty to our fellow humans has to have come from God, the Lord of love and justice.

There's something in this. It would make sense, as image-bearers, that we have an echo in our post-Fallen broken souls, of God's original design and purpose. In his sovereignty and providence, we continue to exercise it, perhaps even unknowingly. As Christians, however, we have been given no uncertain instructions that we absolutely should exercise it.

Behavioral science and social psychology is a modern field of research that is looking into questions that now shed even more light on God's amazing plans for us.[18] Stefan Klein in his book *Survival of the Nicest: How Altruism Made Us Human, and Why it Pays to Get Along* posits the question about why humans display any altruistic tendencies. After all, if helping others makes you more successful, evolution ought to favor that behavior.

He notes, that as human beings are fundamentally selfish, altruism flies in the face of this. "*Nature however*", he says, "*has a clever way to get us to do what she wants.*" "Nature," he says, rewards altruistic behavior by making us feel good. In the same way that eating produces pleasure, doing good activates the same bits of the brain. But getting us to like

---

[18] That's not the point of the research but as with all fields, as we discover more, we are shown more about God's amazing design.

eating (some of us a bit too much) is aimed at storing up fat for the lean times (thanks primal instincts). What does altruism achieve?

It achieves a working community. Communities just don't work if every action's only aim is to benefit that individual. We are wired to live in community. Altruism doesn't necessarily benefit the individual per se, but it benefits the group, which then protects the individual.

But scientists are also finding that acts of altruism can prevent or alleviate depression, so there is still a direct personal benefit. The side benefit or by-product of an instinct to make community work, is our incentive for doing it in the first place – making us feel good.

Now, as Christians, we can read this and say "well, durr". Of course we are wired to live in community. We know it from Genesis.

It also comes as no surprise to me that altruism makes us feel good. When, with my church, we stepped out in faith to form relationships with various groups in our community (a women's domestic violence refuge and a soup kitchen), we would all trot along feeling like we were doing God's work and high-fiving each other in our good-and-faithful-servant-ness. It felt like we had passed a test even going. When we got to these places, we were so changed. The first time I went to the women's refuge, I cried all afternoon afterwards. Not because I was horrified by what I had seen (but don't get me wrong, it was extremely confronting) but because I was so grateful to God for taking me there and placing me where we could shine even a tiny bit of light in the darkest of places.

Doing things like that changes you. It stretches you. It grows you. It makes you see God in the most unlikely places. But it makes you see that he is everywhere.

And it makes you feel good. I know how that must sound. I don't mean it was fun. I don't mean it was a touristy day out. I mean we went, we saw, we were shocked, we adapted, we did what was needed, we did it with, and by, God's grace and we learned.

God gave us a heart to step out in faith and meet those women. By

God's great grace we returned there regularly for the next 4 years. And each time we felt the same joyful gratitude – the satisfaction of being God's hands and feet.

Making a difference feels good, so it's an encouragement to do it more. But I think there is more complexity to blessing others that is a deliberate piece of God's plans. Doing God's work is deeply satisfying – it is satisfying in and of itself. It might not start that way. It might start as "that thing you know you ought to do". It might start as a thing you sort of got guilted into because there weren't enough people. It might have started as something you thought would be kind of cool, but also would make you look pretty good. It might even have started as something that you got into by accident. But as you minister to people in your team, working together for God's purposes, the task becomes satisfying in and of itself. The fear, the discomfort, the self-interest, the boredom all fade into the background. When you throw yourself into God's work, you become intrigued by the people you interact with, you start seeing them as people – God's creation – instead of a group of unknown random people. Your eyes are opened to new things, new ideas, things you would never have known unless God had put you there at that moment. That's when you see God. That's when you understand how detailed and how imminent and how *present* God is in the every day. And that's when your heart swells with the satisfaction that only comes from faithful service.

This shouldn't really be a surprise to us. As God's people we already know the difference in how we feel on our more obedient days and our less obedient days. I know that when I start the day with Bible reading and prayer the day goes better. On a grander scale, the Bible gives us example on example of people who are blessed with contentment in their obedience, and those who live anxious and jarring lives of disobedience. We only need to look to Jonah to see how he resists doing God's work and what discomfort it brings him.

And yet when we are obedient, we don't just achieve some kind of mental equilibrium, God pours out blessing in abundance. Deuteronomy 28:1-13 describes in detail the level of abundance that God promises as his response to the Israelites obedience to his commands. Throughout Deuteronomy, the commands God gives to Moses include a great many that involve a gracious, just and compassionate approach to the working of the society and the community, including care for the poor and for those who are foreigners (c.f. 10:19, 15:11 and 24:19).

The blessings that God relays to Moses in Deuteronomy 28 appear very alien to us – they relate to crops and calves and kneading troughs. It is descriptive, however, not prescriptive. It does not prescribe that only those with kneading troughs and calves will be blessed. It describes, through visual imagery, the kinds of blessings God will pour out. For example, it says they will be blessed in the city and countryside. This is a device of Hebrew poetry to describe the limits of space – so the Israelites will be blessed everywhere. There follows a series of couplets that read like a swift paced list to emphasize the extent of God's blessing:

The fruit of your womb will be blessed, and the crops of your land and the young of your livestock—the calves of your herds and the lambs of your flocks. (verse 4)

(The blessing will reach to the next generation.)

Your basket and your kneading trough will be blessed. (verse 5)

(Everything you do with your hands will be blessed.)

You will be blessed when you come in and blessed when you go out. (verse 6)

(You will be blessed everywhere at every time… and so on.)

The picture that is built is one of abundant and enduring gifts from God in the life of the obedient. I do not mean this to sound like material or financial blessings because this passage in Deuteronomy does not (nor any other part of scripture) promise riches and wealth in return for obedience. It might be one of the blessings, who knows? But that's not what it's getting at. The passage builds a holistic picture of blessing as a total package, as a contented life.

I can say that after a session working with the women at the Refuge, I felt blessed in enormous abundance.

We are wired to feel good when we bless others There appear to be logical reasons for that in our evolutionary biology. Communities work better when altruism is one of the building blocks. But when someone jumps onto train tracks at the risk of their own lives without even a conscious thought, *I* believe that comes from God. I believe it comes from God because that instinct seems counter-intuitive, even in the context of evolutionary biology. I believe it comes from God because he has wired us so clearly to feel immense satisfaction in even the simplest good deeds.

We can know this drive to bless others comes from God, because he told us many times in the pages of the Bible. My point here is that we see his blessings play out in our experience. These blessings are available to us every day and if your spirits are flagging, this will fill you up.

John Piper has often said that God is most glorified in us when we are most satisfied in him. There is a beautiful tangibility to our relationship with God in this. God by his enormous mercy saved us. When we are obedient, he blesses us abundantly which we can feel strongly in our hearts and minds. It gives us satisfaction, a joy in doing kingdom work – and so we glorify God through our joyful toil, which means that others around us can truly see God's light being shined through the deeds that he purposes us to do.

Blessings others also takes the focus off ourselves

Amazing things happen when you bless someone else like you give yourself hot chocolate. Suddenly you are fulfilling your potential. Suddenly you see God everywhere. Suddenly there's a fire in your belly.

You see God's love in action. It makes everything real. No matter how busy you are, there is always someone you can bless.

Make time to serve others. You could volunteer at a soup kitchen, at a shelter, find a church that has a mission to the homeless, or volunteer at a mobile pantry or food bank. You can knit or crochet blankets and beanies for the homeless. You can collect for care packages for the needy.

Seek people out. Meet them. Take care of their material and spiritual needs.

Do it once. Do it every month. Get to know the people you are serving. Pray for them. I guarantee you will make their lives better, even though it might not look like it. And I guarantee it will lift your heart to God and give you a passion for his glory.

Ask yourself, What can I do? Not in the negative (there are so many poor – what can I possibly do?). Ask What can I *do*? I have this much time, what can I do with it? Pray about it. "God – what do you want me to do with my time? There will always be poor in this land. But I have time. And I have a heart for Jesus. I can do something." And whatever that something is, it will glorify God and show others who he is. God told us point blank he wants us to do it. Jesus modelled what we were to do. There is sacrifice involved. Not death, obviously, but time, effort, energy. Blessing others is not meant to be convenient. If I only bless people when it's convenient to me, it's not a sacrifice and it glorifies nobody.

God even wired us to want to do it. How clever is that? I mean seriously, I know God is pretty amazing all round, but how *clever* is that??

Show people God. They may even join you on the journey.

Chapter 10
Keeping Our Eyes Fixed On Jesus

What I think I should be doing:
I will always remember the big picture and keep my eyes fixed on Jesus

What I really think about what I should be doing:
I don't know what this really means

The Proposition

I always feel energized when I hear the exhortation to keep my eyes fixed on Jesus. But later, alone in the quietness I feel confused. What does keeping my eyes fixed on him actually look like? This is one of those things that I know I'm supposed to do, but I don't really know how.

In this final chapter, we'll look at this concept in terms of cleaning out our brains and making space for the right things. Remember the boat that started with a shiny hull in Chapter 1 but needed a good scrub down once in a while to get rid of the barnacles and algae slowing it down? This clean up is kind of like that but from the inside out.

We have so much mental real estate taken up by other things, that we don't even have the brain space to focus on things we really ought to focus on. This will hopefully give us a final push to feel confident and energized to keep going on our journey – not because we're in charge of getting ourselves there, but because we can make choices about things along the way. And these choices affect how we do our journey.

Mental spring cleaning

One of the jobs I like the least in my life is cleaning out the fridge. It happens about every month. There are some congealing jars of curry paste that I used for one meal and then never used again. There's leftover lettuce and zucchini that are cultivating penicillin in the salad drawers and there are several tubs of (now) unidentifiable leftovers.

What is the reason I clean out the fridge? Because it's a bio-hazard? Because I'm a domestic goddess? I wish. I do it because it needs to be done. I do it because generally the state of my fridge reflects the state of my life – organized or disorganized. I do it because the fridge cleaning fairy is not going to do it for me.

I find the same with my car. The kids empty their school bags on our trips home and I get coffee on the way to work and open mail while I'm at the traffic lights. Before you know it, the car doesn't need to be cleaned so much as excavated.

Sometimes our relationships work the same way. I often find with the kids that I can spend days telling them to do this and not do that, be here and go there – after a while our relationship feels like the equivalent of furry veggies at the bottom of the fridge. That's the time to go to the park or the movies. That's the time to take it back to basics and remember what my relationship with them is all about. It's about helping them feel trust and love and support. It's about letting them just be kids and it's about just letting me be their mum.

Does your spiritual life feel like this sometimes? Do you feel like you're being places and doing things because you've got to? Do you read your Bible because you're supposed to, but flick through the words without really thinking because there's ironing to do for tomorrow? Do you go to church because you'll feel bad if you're not there? Do you avoid going to church events and prayer mornings because you can't handle another thing in the calendar or might be asked to serve?

This is not a chapter about how we should all do more. This is about how we feel about it. This is about taking care of our spiritual life because it is precious and how we *feel* about our spiritual life, reflects the *state* of our spiritual life.

Things mount up. Life gets hard. It just does. When things are busy though, when all those plates are spinning, we feel like we just need to keep our heads down and crack on until... until what? What is it we're waiting for? For things to get easier? I think deep down we all know life is always like this. There's always that extra thing that makes our season harder – that school exam year, that change of job year, that moving house year, that caring for a sick parent year, that having a baby year, that pandemic year! All our things are important and valid. I don't mean to suggest that they're not. I'm just saying that we always have something like that. Life is always like this. We should embrace and accept it and not hunker down hoping things will be easier next year. Next year there will be something else, something wonderful or tragic or difficult, but something else there will be.

When we hunker down, we're allowing the tubs of leftovers to build up, we're allowing the cheese to go off, we're allowing the jars in the fridge door to go sticky. We're not taking care of something that is really precious.

This doesn't mean that we must frantically clear out our spiritual lives all the time. I'm saying that sometimes, just like the fridge, our spiritual life needs a good deep clean so we can keep operating as normal the rest of the time. Just like nobody else will clean my fridge for me, I don't think we can expect our spiritual life to stay on track if we don't do something about it every so often. We can keep it ticking over, sure, and that's important. But we also sometimes need to slap on the rubber gloves and get in there with some bleach and a scrubbing brush.

The Price of Forgetfulness

The Old Testament is such a gold mine. The long history of God's chosen people, continually bungling their spiritual lives. We see the best of people, and we see the worst of them. From 2 Kings 18 particularly we see how easily and quickly God disappeared completely. In 2 Kings 18, Hezekiah becomes King of Judah and he "*did what was right in the eyes of the Lord*" (2 Kings 18:3). So far so good. Like any normal human, Hezekiah had a pretty up and down time of things, more up than down seemingly, but when he died, everything changed. In 2 Kings 21 we see Hezekiah's son Manasseh become king. He reigned for 55 years and "*He did evil in the eyes of the Lord, following the detestable practices of the nations the Lord had driven out before the Israelites.*" (2 Kings 21:2) Manasseh re-built lots of pagan altars and temples – he even put a carved Asherah pole (a significant pagan symbol) in the temple in Jerusalem itself, the place where God had said he would never send his people into the wilderness again if only they would keep the Law of Moses. "*But the people did not listen. Manasseh led them astray, so that they did more evil than the nations the Lord had destroyed before the Israelites.*" (2 Kings 21:9)

Let's just stop here a moment. When I think about "evil" being done in the eyes of God, I'm thinking devil worship, blood sacrifice, big Hollywood finale scenes where the heroine is saved just before her heart is cut out etc. etc. Probably not so dramatic but there may be something in this – the Canaanite pagan practices did involve animal worship (1 Kings 18:23) and sometimes children (Deuteronomy 12:31) and there was sex too (1 Kings 14:23-24).

Let's think about how this would look for your ordinary guy though.

We read 2 Kings and it all happens so fast we think it must all have happened instantaneously. But all Manasseh's religious changes must have taken place over a period of time – it's not like he could have done it all on Day 1. Nobody stopped him though. At least not that the Bible tells us. He was the king and you go along with what he does, right? He led them astray – again, something that happens over a process of time.

Fifty-five years is not that long to lead a country astray. It's within living memory. At the time of writing, 55 years ago would be 1963. Think about how different our world is since then. There's been the Civil Rights movement, the Nixon era, the Berlin Wall, the rise of feminism, the Arab-Israeli conflict, and the space race – and that's just in the 60s.

At the other end, think about how our lives have changed in the last few years. Think about every "newfangled thing" that came along that now is integral to your life. Less than 10 years ago, I did not get the point of Facebook at all. Now it's how I do most of my work in communicating with ministry teams and contacts. It started small, it was gradual and I barely noticed how significant it was becoming in my life. It was championed by the influencers and trendsetters of the day and I just followed the crowd.

After Manasseh, Amon ruled for just 2 years and then came Josiah. This guy was the bomb. He did right in the eyes of the Lord. But it wasn't until the 18th year of his reign that he decided to give the temple in Jerusalem a little fixer upper, during which they "found" the Book of the Law (2 Kings 22:8). They found it? So it was lost? Josiah had never heard it. When he did, he tore his robes in anguish. It was read to all the people and they repented and renewed their pledge to the covenant. Good outcome. But that's how quickly the "led astray" had happened. In the space of less than one lifetime, the *entire Bible* (as it was back then) was forgotten.

We cannot be those people. We are just as sinful and frail and broken and prone to wander. So we need to take care of our spiritual life – what we choose to avoid today, could be the price of forgetfulness tomorrow.

Re-remember the basics

When I spring-clean my fridge, I just keep the basics. Usually the butter, milk and eggs. I only throw out what has deteriorated over time and needs to be discarded. Sometimes we look at the basics and think "Boring!" Like when we hear the gospel (again). I've heard that, you think. I know that backwards.

But isn't this the very thing we need to re-remember? Isn't this the thing we need to clean all the dirt away to expose? Paul wrote to the Corinthians to do just that:

"Now, brothers and sisters, I want to remind you of the gospel I preached to you, which you received and on which you have taken your stand. By this gospel you are saved, if you hold firmly to the word I preached to you. Otherwise, you have believed in vain.

For what I received I passed on to you as of first importance: that Christ died for our sins according to the Scriptures, that he was buried, that he was raised on the third day according to the Scriptures, and that he appeared to Cephas, and then to the Twelve. After that he appeared to more than five hundred of the brothers and sisters at the same time, most of whom are still living, though some have fallen asleep." (1 Corinthians 15:1-6)

This passage is generally agreed by super smart university type people to be a creedal statement that Paul has imported into his letter. By creed I mean a clear statement of the things we believe that can be memorized and repeated by believers as a reminder of the truths we hold to.

They (the super smart people) think it is a creedal statement because of how Paul introduces it. He says what he received he passed on and the terms used in the original New Testament writing have rabbinic equivalent terms for passing on of tradition. So if a rabbi was using terms for passing on a set tradition, these are the "received" and "passing on" terms he'd use. And these are the terms that Paul uses here.

It's also the style of it – *That* Christ died for our sins... *That* he was buried... *That* he was raised on the third day... *That* he appeared to Cephas... and so on. It's not a normal way of speaking and has a certain formula that is consistent with creedal statements.

Great. Why is this even important?

Well, all this means that this is something found in early Christian culture, outside of Paul's own words that he's now using.

This is the voice of the early church speaking.

On top of that – Paul received it before he passed it on, so scholars almost unanimously believe that this creed pre-dates Paul. Most date it no later than the mid-40s AD. How crazy is that? They think it's a verbal formula that is dated as potentially one of the earliest things we know about Christianity.

Here's a quick history lesson.

- Jesus was born approximately 3-ish BC and was crucified about 30AD.
- Paul was converted in around 33 or 34AD, and in Galatians Paul says he heard the gospel from Jesus, and from no other man.
- Then he went up to Jerusalem about 3 years after his conversion – so 36 or 37AD to meet with Peter and James and the Jerusalem church.

We don't know what they talked about but we have to assume they would have discussed the gospel and what Paul was doing.

At this time there was lots of movement of Christians after the early persecution that we read about in the book of Acts. If you remember from Acts 7, Stephen is stoned to death and the Christians scatter from

Jerusalem all over the Roman world. A creedal statement was the easiest and clearest way of affirming that believers were on the same page. So it's entirely believable that this would be an incredibly early verbal statement and Paul could have received this creed at around this time.

But whether the creed was dated to about 37AD or the mid-40s, this means the creed is set within 5-10 years of the crucifixion. Now this is astonishing. Here we see the set belief of all Christians – who at this time and ongoing from this time – are poor, persecuted, imprisoned, and murdered. This statement is the same in essence as the ones we ourselves say today.

And notice Paul says that the risen Jesus appeared to 500 people! Many of them have died but many are still alive at the time of writing to the Corinthians – this creed is *checkable*. And these eyewitnesses are the ones in danger and they are swearing to it as truth – it's not something they would spread around lightly.

Stephen had already been stoned to death (after which a persecution broke out). Philip was scourged and killed by the Romans 54AD – about the time of the letter to the Corinthians. Peter had been imprisoned in Jerusalem at the beginning of Acts and Paul and Barnabas themselves are under threat as they do their missionary work.

Why would they do this unless they held to a common belief that they believed was true? A truth believed not because someone told them, but believed because they *saw* it.

These are the basics. And it's not ho-hum. It's not ordinary and boring. It's *extraordinary*. People who were there and were witness to the events died for following Jesus. And what's more, this creed appeared so early after the events, there was no time for it to have evolved and been shaped over years. If that had been the case, it would have been too hard for everyone to have the same knowledge simultaneously once they were scattered to the winds. No. This creed was created at the source – in

Jerusalem – and then scattered with the persecuted Christians. This is not something that evolved over time, this has always been the truth.

Paul wrote it to remind the Corinthians of what they believe. That's what he says in 15:1. Why would he need to remind them unless they were forgetting? Just like the Israelites in the Old Testament, our inclination is to be distracted by what's in front of us and what's around us. We need to be reminded of the basics. And we need to be reminded of how absolutely extraordinary it is. When we take ourselves "out for a service" we are giving ourselves time and space to re-remember these truths and ponder at their wonder.

What grows us in our faith is not exciting party atmospheres and standing alongside hundreds or thousands of Christian brothers and sisters (although both are great for a cracking conference!). What grows us is the truth of the gospel, heard afresh, and which lays the foundations for teaching that then fertilizes our growth in Christ-likeness and strengthens our discipleship.

Making space in our week

God rested on the seventh day, the day that became the Sabbath. This is the biblical concept of rest. The Israelites were to work for six days and rest on the seventh, as God had done (Exodus 20:8). Moses fleshed out the concept to say it was to remember that they were slaves in Egypt and that they were saved by God (Deuteronomy 5:15). This Sabbath was a day of rest and remembrance – to remember what God made, and what God did. This day of rest and reflection became twisted into a list of things that couldn't be done, things that counted as "work" and were therefore forbidden. These included things like writing, shopping, doing laundry (although I'm a big fan of this prohibition), using the telephone, driving, cooking, gardening and turning on and off anything that uses electricity. What God gave us as a blessing, humans minimized into a list of do's and don'ts.

The Westminster Confession of Faith, written in 1646 and still a foundation of Protestant doctrine today, outlines in Chapter 21, section 8:

This Sabbath is then kept holy unto the Lord, when men, after a due preparing of their hearts, and ordering of their common affairs beforehand, do not only observe a holy rest, all the day, from their own works, words, and thoughts about their worldly employments and recreations, but also are taken up, the whole time, in the public and private exercises of his worship, and in the duties of necessity and mercy.

This, to me, has a beautiful focus on the heart and preparing for time spent with God. God himself in Exodus 20:8 had said to keep the day holy, that is, set apart. It must be different to the other days of the week. It has a different purpose.

I remember when I was a kid, even though I grew up in a non-religious house, no shops were open on a Sunday. There'd be little noise and no traffic or the general hubbub of the normal working weekdays. Culturally, Sunday was still the day of observance. You didn't shop or work or do big projects or do sports. In those days it was easier to keep the day set apart, even for non-Christians. There wasn't even opportunity to do anything. Now, Sunday to me seems indistinguishable from any other day of the week. All the shops are open, as well as the cafes and restaurants, pubs and kids' activities. Sunday has become the extension of Saturday. Whatever you don't get to do on Saturday, you can do on a Sunday. Or, even more modern an attitude, Saturday is our day to rest and do sports, and Sunday is for chores and shopping and all the work that's needed around the home.

We have no real cultural memory anymore of how to "do" Sunday.

We are not the first era of people for whom this was an issue. This was also the case back in the 17th century. This was the century in

England that saw the death of Elizabeth I after 45 years on the throne, and by the middle of the century a Civil War ripped the country apart along social, political and religious lines. This is the era that saw the rise of the Puritans. We know these people as the big hat and big collar guys who hated fun and loved austerity. In actual fact, the Puritans were the Reformed Evangelicals of the day. They were devout, no question, but this was in comparison to the fun loving new post-Elizabethan crowd. Under the new Stuart regime, church was a necessary good, but not to be taken too literally, and which should be kept safely formulaic. The Puritans believed in prayer and personal devotions and a life lived as sacrificial worship to God and a personal relationship with Jesus. Sound familiar? The Puritans gave us the writings and pastoral ministry of John Owen, Richard Baxter and Matthew Henry. If you aren't familiar with these guys or the Puritans, I highly recommend them to you.[19]

Anyway, for the Stuart-era people, Sundays were for a bit of church but mostly fun and sports. For the Puritans, Sunday was an entire day set aside and devoted to church gathering, prayer, worship, discussion and meditation. Their day was a Sabbath, set apart and dedicated to God to appreciate what God made, and remember what he did. The "rest" of the Sabbath was resting in God.

I'm not big on reducing our Sabbath rest to a list of do's and don'ts. But wouldn't it be interesting if we were more intentional about our Sunday and tried to live it out in a way that honored God's intent for the day? Going to church is good as a solid anchor-point for the week, but apart from that – rest and reflection can take many forms. Reading, family time, time with friends, relaxing, hospitality, gardening, whatever it is, undertaken through the lens of God's wishes for us. Then whatever the day holds, the motivation to be conscious of God is the key.

---

[19] J. I. Packer's books *Puritan Portraits* and *A Quest for Godliness* are great start points for learning about the Puritans.

If the day is for God and not for us/everyone else, maybe it would help us to make some choices about things we don't need to do that day. Maybe it would help us to slow things down and, by not treating it like a Saturday, help us to find the breathing space we need.

God gave us the concept of the Sabbath as a blessing – it was a day of rest, a time to rest in him. Many of us see Sunday as *our* day. Many of us even see church as "my time". What if we see it as *God's* day? This can be difficult for us. After a hard week at work and then taking care of all the things that need to be squeezed into a Saturday, I can imagine that many might roll their eyes at the thought of giving their Sunday to God. I'm not saying we sacrifice it begrudgingly. That would be a very poor offering to God. What I mean is willingly and joyfully offering the day up to God. Being at church – not just going but being at church, being there for the church community. And then the rest of the day given over to hospitality or meals with Christian brothers and sisters, or intentional family time centered around Jesus.

I suspect that if we offered our Sabbath time to God, we would find it an enormous blessing to ourselves. Because that's how God works. It's wonderful, isn't it?

Making room in our brains

But what about the rest of the time? If we are going to be able to keep going on this journey, we can't limit our God-ward focused brains to just a Sunday church service and a Bible study. If we do, we won't be able to maintain the stamina to keep going, or we'll hamper ourselves with unnecessary and unhelpful thoughts.

Most of the things that clutter my brain are worries. Things that I said, how I said it, things I didn't say, things someone said to me, things they didn't say but implied, things I did, things I should have done but didn't... sound familiar? I can suppress things like that most of the time, but when the lights go off at the end of the day, suddenly there they all are – things that I can't change, but things I can't seem to stop worrying about.

Worry is, in itself, sinful. Because it keeps a focus on ourselves and things we can't change and diverts our focus from our sovereign God who is in charge of all things. If we worry about something, what we are really doing is not believing that God has got it under control. This is obviously easy to say. Worry is a very natural thing and kicks in without us even realizing.

"Humble yourselves, therefore, under God's mighty hand, that he may lift you up in due time. Cast all your anxiety on him because he cares for you." (1 Peter 5:6-7) Most inspirational memes stop there. The next bit is key though, *"Be alert and of sober mind. Your enemy the devil prowls around like a roaring lion looking for someone to devour."* (1 Peter 6:8)

When Peter says cast your cares on God, he isn't saying "Because God is really nice n'that", he is saying it because it's an act of humility. He is saying that we harbor worry and we need to let it go, because it gets in the way. We listen to our worries more than we listen to God and, by definition, that makes worrying a temptation to sin. But he's also saying it to keep us safe. Because if we are distracted from God by focusing on our worries, this is where the devil has opportunity to lead us astray.

I have some of my most interesting conversations with young adults. Their perspectives are so fresh and their ideas can be so clear. I learn an awful lot from 18 to 28-year-olds. I spoke to one girl who was facing a series of trials – exams, a death in the family, the loss of two of her beloved pets within two weeks of each other and some big life-changing decisions to make. She was raw and honest in her approach and displayed fantastic self-awareness. She said she felt like this was the first time she'd really had to rely on God in the face of hardship. She felt like, up until now, she'd never really had to rely on him for anything that serious – she'd never been tested in the fire. So even though her faith was strong, she felt exposed and vulnerable. The lion prowls around, and she felt like the gazelle on the edges of the herd – the one that looks easiest to pick off.

This is what worries do. They make us exposed and vulnerable. So we need, for our spiritual safety, to deal with them, and manage them. But worry is not something you can easily get rid of. You can't just switch it off. And I am sure that there are people reading this for whom worry and anxiety is something far more dark and debilitating. These issues can be like having any physical issue. Asthma doesn't go away, but we manage it. Arthritis will always be there, but there are ways that we can deal with it on an ongoing basis. Worry is just the same.

Thankfully for us, we have a God who wants us to rest our bodies and minds so that we can focus on him, and in so doing, make ourselves stronger and more able to do what he purposes for us, and run the race to the end.

Falling in love with Jesus

Falling in love is amazing. We all remember our first love. The adrenaline, the excitement, the anticipation, the feeling of wanting to be with them all the time, the yearning to know them more, the longing for the future as you write yourself into a story together and imagine it, and rehearse and replay it in your head.

Being in love activates all the dopamine centers of the brain. We've talked about dopamine before – it's the reward center of the brain. This would be why those feelings of anticipation are so pleasurable and exciting.

This is where our journey as Christians began. There are differences and complexity and nuances, but we fell in love. For me, it was my brain first. On balance, all the information in front of me seemed more likely to be true than not. As my knowledge grew, so did my passion for Christ.

About a year after my "head" conversion, it clicked in my heart too and I fell deeply in love. Not romantic love, a different kind of love for my God and my King, my Lord and my Savior, my friend and my father. It was a love filled with awe and reverence and gratitude. There were no visions or dreams or anything. It was a deep and certain knowledge.

Some people have never had that. Some people had bells and whistles and fireworks right from the beginning. Some people have grown up Christian and never had an epiphany like I was expecting. Some people just *know* and have never had a defining moment where they started to believe. All of our experiences with the risen Christ are personal and unique and wonderful, and one is not better or more valid than another. Whether it's an exciting story or a really ordinary story, it's special. Nobody's story is boring. Never think that for a second. And as a side note for anyone reading this who thinks their story is boring because they have never wrestled with doubt or had a great awakening or had a dream or a vision – please know that your experience is exactly what I pray for my kids every day, and I'll bet it's what your parents prayed for you too!

But love is love. It's a term much used and abused, but what I mean is, it's an emotion that is a wonderful gift from God and that is vulnerable to us humans mucking it up. We fall in love (whether with bells and whistles or with quiet certainty) and then we expect it to stay the same. This goes for relationships between humans as much as it does between us and God. Our relationship can't be sustained at the level it was when we first realized the depth of our sin and the magnitude of God's grace. We can remember it and feel it again and know it for sure in our minds, but we can't put our faith in our feelings.

In a human relationship, apparently it takes 12-18 months to "normalize". What that means is that the dopamine levels come back to normal and that dizzy excitement smooths out. This is where the real work begins with a relationship. It's where a relationship gets comfortable. You maybe don't feel the need to be with that person *all the time*. Maybe, you start seeing things that you don't like or irritate you a bit. Sometimes, you start taking them for granted a little bit.

We know this happens in life. We know this happens with our relationship with God – it's the reason for this book. At the beginning everything is more exciting. As time moves on, how do you stand fast? How do you keep your eyes fixed on Jesus? How do you maintain a relationship with a spouse, let alone the God of the universe? In fact, with the God of the universe it may even be harder, because it requires bending your mind around huge concepts that can't be seen. A spouse is right in front of you. You can see them and they talk back when you speak to them. You can go for dinner and have a laugh. God can be very difficult to get your arms and your mind around. All of who he is and what he can do is more than we can grasp. The feelings wain. The relationship anchor points (going to church and Bible study etc.) become cumbersome and dull.

Now, we've spoken about a lot of these things already. But there's a reason that our relationship with God is the final chapter. Our relationship with God in one sense, *is* the destination. We have started the journey with God. We're in his car, and it's the best place to be – just like the disciples were in the boat the night of the storm in Mark 4:35-41.

In another sense, we still have this road to travel, because while we are with God now, we still aren't there yet. We still have work to do. And that's hard. But we know that any relationship that is going to work takes effort. We can't just put the car on cruise control and then stop steering. If we did, we'd be off the road at the first bend.

It's the same with a relationship. If we stop trying, all ends badly.

This whole book has grappled with ways that we can re-energize various aspects of our relationship with God and re-calibrate our lives in a God-ward direction. But at the heart of it all *is* the relationship with

God. And it's fitting that we end here, with this most central element of our faith.

How do we bring this all together?

The early editor adding the section title to Hebrews 11 describes the lives and behaviors of Abel, Enoch, Noah, Abraham, Isaac, Jacob, Joseph, Moses and Rahab as "faith in action". They were on the other side of the cross from us. They didn't know what the plan was supposed to be. They just knew what God told them, they acted on it, and by the time they died, they hadn't seen how the plan was to play out. We have the benefit of living by faith in Jesus, the image of God. We have someone to guide us. They had nothing like it. Theirs was hard core faith.

"These were all commended for their faith, yet none of them received what had been promised, since God had planned something better for us so that only together with us would they be made perfect.

Therefore, since we are surrounded by such a great cloud of witnesses, let us throw off everything that hinders and the sin that so easily entangles. And let us run with perseverance the race marked out for us, fixing our eyes on Jesus, the pioneer and perfecter of faith. For the joy set before him he endured the cross, scorning its shame, and sat down at the right hand of the throne of God." (Hebrews 11:39-12:2)

God's promises have always centered around a time and place where his chosen people will live with him in eternity. What the pre-Christ believers got was an imperfect picture of living in the Promised Land (Canaan). An echo of what the new heaven and new earth would be. They lived with God dwelling with them, in the tabernacle and the temple, but not a shade close to living with him always and eternally.

The apocalyptic picture of heaven in Revelation 21 and 22 is amazing. People often ask if that is what heaven will actually look like.

I don't know. It could be a heavily symbolized description of a generally good place, but not an actual description of actual heaven. It may be what heaven will look like, using phrases and descriptors from our puny language to describe something so perfect and heavenly we only have words that can approximate it. One thing we know is it's going to be good. The other thing we know is that we'll live there with God. And perhaps that's as far as we need to go. Anything beyond that is speculative and can be a bit of a side show, when we haven't been given enough information to pin it down and draw a picture.

In Genesis 3:8, after Adam and Eve have eaten the fruit of the tree of knowledge, there is a picture of God given *"as he was walking in the garden in the cool of the day."* I love this. It could be real. It could be an anthropomorphized description (given a human form and behavior to help us understand the concept of God's presence). Either way, I love this feeling that God wandered among his creation to appreciate all his good works. I like to think heaven will be like this. Where God wanders among his creation to appreciate it beauty and diversity.

All the characters in Hebrews 11 have not had the benefit of the security we have in Jesus though. They just had to trust. But God knew, that together *with us*, it would all come to perfection. They are our witnesses. We can look to them to draw inspiration and encouragement. They can spur us on like a cheer squad on the side of the road. And we can draw comfort from them, because they did it without Jesus. *We have Jesus.*

The rest of this passage in Hebrews, gives us great advice that we should stop and pick apart. We should throw off everything that hinders. Hinders in the original Greek is ὄγκον or *ogkon* and describes something that is a burden or a great weight. Imagine trying to run while carrying a suitcase, or driving while dragging a heavy trailer. It would slow you down, drain your energy, make it difficult to do what you need to do, maybe even make you give up.

What are your suitcases?

Maybe there are some things you need to reduce or leave behind to make the journey easier to complete. Are there things that get in the way, or slow you down? Are you doing too much of something? Are you carrying burdens from your pre-Christian life? Friends that hold you back? Groups you are trying to fit in with? These are the things that will hinder you and, as hard as it might be, the Bible says to throw all that off.

We are also to throw off the sin that so easily entangles. Here the word is εὐπερίστατον or *euperistaton*. It's something that surrounds you easily, something that would get in the way of you running. Imagine running through a thicket or getting snagged on lantana and trying to keep running. At best you might be held back and sweat and strain to keep going. At worst, you stop. These are not what we think of as "big sins", they're things that we might not imagine are bad in and of themselves. They are things that have surrounded and snagged us.

What are your entangling sins?

Maybe there are little things that you let slow you down. Getting fixated with social media or games, always thinking one more drink will be okay, pushing the boundaries with your TV and media watching, letting your language slip around non-Christians… Maybe it's even allowing yourself to dwell on negative issues or letting your heart mull on things people have done so you cultivate a bitter root there.

We need to look at these things, because the Bible tells us we need to run the race with endurance. Those two things don't seem to go together. Running is a fast thing. Endurance is a steady thing. But we need to do both. This isn't a sprint. It's a marathon. Trying to do a marathon is hard enough without carrying suitcases and being snagged on lantana. It can't be done. The only way to run is to get rid of those things.

The only way to then run steadfastly is to have a mind set for perseverance. We see it all the time on those crash dieting and make-over shows. The people that succeed are the ones that have mental stamina. That's what we need. We can go to church, we can read our Bibles, but if we don't have the mental stamina, it's going to fall flat eventually.

And Hebrews tells us how we get that perseverance. We keep our eyes fixed on Jesus. What's interesting is the word used. The word is ἀφορῶντες or *aphorōntes*. It is the action of turning our eyes away from something else, in order to fix them on a particular object. So if we ever wonder what "fixing our eyes on Jesus" really means in practical terms, it means turning our attention away from all those other things, in order to fix them on him. This will play out in the choices we make, in how we think and how we use our time. It's not just "read your Bible and pray". It is those things obviously, but it is so much more than that. This is not just a journey, this is a relationship. Think of your relationship with God as you would with a person. What holds marriages together? What keeps you close with your kids? How do you build and maintain close friendships? You invest. You engage. You spend time thinking about it. You work on being present in the relationship.

Go back to chapters of this book that might help you in areas that are a particular struggle for you. Read this book with a friend and talk about it. Bring your problems and thoughts and questions and fears into the light. Ask God to help you. Because here's the most amazing thing of all – God wants us to finish this journey. He sent his only son to die for us. And Jesus came so that we might have life and have it to the full. Don't we want to live like that's true?

I need to say again, this is not about a list of do's and don't's. We have been saved by grace. That's all. We will be walking in heaven with our God – and for you reading this, I look forward to meeting you there!

All the things we have talked about in this book are about how we keep growing as a *response* to God's grace. Not how to be saved or how to stay saved. This is about staying strong and helping each other to work on the bits that hold us back. It's about supporting each other to keep our focus and make more room for God as our Christian journey gets hard – or is just tangled in the realness of our day to day lives.

This is a journey. It's a really long journey. But we are in it together. We are in it with God.

> *Do you not know?*
> *Have you not heard?*
> *The Lord is the everlasting God,*
> *the Creator of the ends of the earth.*
> *He will not grow tired or weary,*
> *and his understanding no one can fathom.*
> *He gives strength to the weary*
> *and increases the power of the weak.*
> *Even youths grow tired and weary,*
> *and young men stumble and fall;*
> *but those who hope in the Lord*
> *will renew their strength.*
> *They will soar on wings like eagles;*
> *they will run and not grow weary,*
> *they will walk and not be faint.*
> Isaiah 40:28-31

www.ingramcontent.com/pod-product-compliance
Lightning Source LLC
Chambersburg PA
CBHW070153100426
42743CB00013B/2897